AF345480

# GENTLE LIFE REVISION

ANAND MAHADEVAN

*Foreword By*

COL (DR) PVGS JAYARAM

*Published by*

**Office :** D-328, Defence Colony, New Delhi-110024
**Mobiles:** +91-9810539784, +91-9833283155
**Emails:** ganivpanjrath@yahoo.co.in, tannaazirani@gmail.com



ISBN-13: 9788194978299

ISBN 10: 81-949782-9-7

Printed at Thomson Press, New Delhi

# Note From The Author

I wish to invite my Readers to identify with a near practical life experience while reading this book. The aim of this book is to help the Reader to pause, reflect, find a deeper connect, have an overview of essential reflections in life; and to find guidance in one's eternal journey from life to death, along with a general awareness of basic issues that affect all of us.

The illustrations are simple, practical and have universal applicability. I have attempted to organize, compile and add thoughts about reality as I perceive it through my senses. The aspects covered are factual and perceptual.

I had a long-felt desire to reach out to people in a simple and pragmatic manner to bring about positive changes and deeper understanding in their lives. I have attempted to give the Reader a glimpse of a scenario, wherein, they are given a choice of how their life should look and the knowledge and ability to fix issues or problems if they are able to. This book touches upon a sum of all our experiences.

You can connect with the contents of this Book at whatever stage of life you are in. It is a digest that one may like to keep a copy of. The content has been organized under practical headings which gives the book an apt and meaningful presentation. You can dig deeper into areas that may interest you.

This work is a step towards bringing about a reality check in people's lives and is an attempt to reach out to a large audience. Some basic awareness about a Human life, along with 'Can Do', 'Do not Forget', kind of insights all rolled into and organized in one place, in a distinctive format, to provide a gentle piece of reading.

There is something for everyone here. I consider myself a seeker too, looking for answers to some of my queries though the medium of this book. Connect with the situations in their respective context and find your answers. Take what is best for you.  Each one of us must live healthy, be happy and leave a positive footprint in life's journey.

Find your direction and create the life of your dreams. Develop survival and problem-solving techniques and discover your own spirituality.

Do enjoy going through your simple routine in the journey of life. You can revert to chapters you may feel more relevant to yourself and your dear ones. I hope this essence of life as depicted in a nutshell will make a fine read. Do give me your valuable feedback which, I can incorporate in my future editions.

Reflect back on your life, have a feel of it! Join me on a gentle life revision. Happy Reading.

You may interact with me on the following platforms:

| | |
|---|---|
| ✓ *E mail* | : anandmwriter@gmail.com |
| ✓ *Twitter* | : @colanand5 |
| ✓ *LinkedIn* | : m-anand-1b67851b |
| ✓ *Facebook* | : amdvl11 |
| ✓ *Instagram* | : amdvl11 |
| ✓ *Star Maker* | : anandm_star385 |
| ✓ *You Tube Channel* | : Life Management with Anand |

# *Acknowledgements*

This work is a product of my thoughts, collection and compilation of important knowledge from various sources, and analysis – packaged in my desired format.

This Book would not have been possible without the grace of the Almighty and profound blessings of my parents. My father Major M Mahadevan now a retired Army Veteran and a super senior citizen took immense pains and efforts to raise us providing for the best possible education. He had procured the 'Better English' series of books from England in the seventies, kept us always ahead of the times and was undoubtedly my role model. My mother Vasanthy, a housewife, instilled in us a good value system and ethics and always prayed for the happiness and prosperity of our family. I owe every bit of my success to them.

My special thanks to Ganiv Chadha Panjrath of Creative Crows Publishers LLP who reposed faith in me and constantly encouraged me to accomplish my work.

My overwhelming thanks to Tannaaz Irani, the Chief Editor who was very patient, extremely professional, creative and I got to learn a lot from her.

My gratitude to Dr Kavitha Rajamannikam (MD), my cousin, and her husband Dr Parathan Karunakaran (MD, DM) who were gracious enough to peruse portions related to medical science, as enumerated in the book.

My sincere acknowledgement to various books, talks, mobile texts and numerous unidentified sources and to all those who may have contributed, even though anonymously.

To both my well-wishers and my adversaries, you were my real inspiration to write this book. Thank you all.

I am grateful to Almighty God for giving me this opportunity to be of service to humanity.

# Foreword

It is my singular privilege to have been invited to give the Foreword. I have known the Author for past 25 years and always found him inspirational and motivating. I was fortunate to have worked closely with him during our service life.

The Book is well conceptualized and written in a one-off classic manner bringing forth the important activities in our life and touching upon the deeper connects.

The Book is designed in such a manner that it is relevant for all age groups. As a reader one feels that tremendous effort has been put in to bring out the relevant aspects in a desired format.

Flipping through the Chapters seems like a trip down the memory lane and a lot of practical points suggested and at many places providing a lot of flexibility to the reader to draw his inferences.

Overall, a must read, a lovely digest everyone would like to keep a copy of. It is a piece of work that is unique, useful and handy with a purpose of bringing success, peace and happiness in people's lives.

Signing off wishing the Author success in all his future works in both nonfiction as well as fiction category.

*Col (Dr) PVGS Jayaram*

**Ministry of Defence**

**New Delhi**

*About Col ( Dr) PVGS JAYARAM*

*Col (Dr) PVGS Jayaram is a technocrat, who excelled in the fields of Radar, Geospatial and Space Technologies; during his experience of over two decades in the Army. The Officer has served in the United Nations as Military Observer & Chief Geospatial Officer. He pro-actively worked with foreign operators in developing Operational Information Systems for the Army.*

*The Officer has Master's degree in Technology and PhD in Spatial Information Technology. He contributes generously in building Technology for National Security. He has published technical papers in International Journals and takes to writing on philosophical subjects and life - lessons as part of his passion.*

As you read along, find
your unique connections
as it suits you best  and
continue to inspire
people around you.


**Anand Mahadevan** ❧

# Table Of Contents

# Chapter 1:
# Introduction

Man is the highest creation of God. Happiness is the highest form of success. There are no riches beyond sound health, and no joy above the joy of mind. Life is a journey and not a race.

Everything is temporary, nothing is permanent. We all must desire to lead happy and fulfilling lives. We must acquire basic knowledge and understanding of Life concepts and be also able to guide others in need.

We all must aim at being physically fit, mentally sound, emotionally healthy and spiritually enlightened.

Human life is a combination of the physical, astral, and casual bodies. The physical body is alone perceptible to our senses. The astral body is formed by the association of the infinitesimal energy particles, and is known as life force. The third one is the casual (magnetic) body or the soul.

The basic human soul is surrounded by sheaths, one above another, the outer ones penetrating the inner ones from the physical body; from the skin inwards to the etheric body which covers and permeates the physical gross body. The last one is said to be located in the heart and is closely related with our inner world called the actual Atman, spirit or soul. The koshas are the metaphorical layers that comprise the human body and mind and house the soul. Yoga philosophy describes the physical body, the subtle body and the casual body as the three bodies that encompass the five koshas. The human body and the life force energy (breath or prana) is part of the physical body, while mind and intellect are included in the subtle body. The casual body is considered as the innermost self or soul, which cycles through birth, death, re birth and ultimately transcendence. Their job is acquisition of knowledge and directing functioning of the body as well as mind, intelligence, ego, consciousness; and five outward senses; also including pain, pleasure and emotions. Breath, that we inhale digests food and directs excretions.

The source of all existence is universal cosmic consciousness which manifests as male and female energy. Both are eternal, timeless and immeasurable and present in all living beings. The five elements namely space, air, fire, water and earth exist in all matter.

These five great elements combine into three basic energies which are present in varying degrees. Space and Air combine as Vata. Fire and Water combine as Pitta. Water and earth constitute Kapha. These humors govern our psychobiological functioning and cause individual differences and preferences. One of them is primary, a proportion uniquely their own, balance being the natural order of things.

We have no control over where we are born or our heritage, but to a large extent we are able to control over what we can do with our lives. Everything in life falls into place when you are in harmony with yourself.

Stay calm and let your life unfold. We are mostly so busy in our lifestyle that we simply don't find the time to keep a check on our activities. We all know what is good or bad for us, yet we can only implement it if we constantly remind ourselves and place it on our priority list as a Reminder.

We need to imbibe course corrections to be close to the standard pattern of being successful and happy in whatever we do. From our birth to death, our destiny is dependent on our reactions and responses to external and internal stimuli. We generally do react to stimuli, pleasant or unpleasant.

Happiness is in what you enjoy doing and not essentially in what you have. The display of power and pride is also temporary and hence false. Each soul has its own journey. Don't judge or injure in thought or action. In a nutshell live as you did as a child; laugh, don't worry, eat when hungry, be active. Remember everything you see today was a dream before it became a reality!

The two foremost challenges are Desire and Healthy Occupation, driven by opposing forces. As a charioteer of your life, steer clear and Behold!

*If you can't fly run, if you can't run walk, if you can't walk crawl, but keep moving*

*-Martin Luther King*

Reach your destination, complete your journey. Endeavor to start your journey with one good thought and one good deed. There will be good days and there will be bad days too. Take it in your stride.

One needs to develop a disciplined life and be disciplined about daily routines without stressing oneself. Know and analyze your strengths and weaknesses.

We live in times of confusion, for simple questions there are tons of complicated answers. Sometimes we need a Guide along our life journey.

Read good books daily, they are Man's best friend, as the old saying goes. Make it a compulsive habit.

You may have to deliver an output that requires more than the usual hours which are at your disposal to be able to achieve greater heights in life; which is also one of the secrets to success in life.

Everyone comes with a baggage, take responsibility for your conditions. Every problem has a solution.

Think positive, talk positive, feel positive. Don't finish in a negative sentence, turn it around and see how it changes your perceptions; never say I can't do it.

We have the power to choose to be the Good, Bad or the Ugly. Walk away from toxic and negative people who hound you in your own nest.

Humans can create their own environment, whereas animals adapt to it.

Very few people live to their true potential. A purposeless life is a living death. Purpose brings passion.

Don't wait to be rich to be happy. Happiness is free. Enjoy every moment of life. Pure bliss and joy are beyond explanation and definition.

A group of people once visited a wise man complaining about the same problem over and over again. One day, he decided to tell them a joke and they all roared with laughter. After a few minutes, he told them the same joke and some of them laughed. After a few minutes, he told them the same joke and only a few of them smiled. Then he told the same joke again, but no one laughed or smiled anymore. The wise man smiled and said, you can't laugh at the same joke over and over. So why do you wish to cry over the same problem repeatedly? Don't relive your past agonies.

Bring Love wherever you go. Judge nothing, you will be happy. It is possible to change the world around us by changing ourselves.

Many times, in life we are at important crossroads. We can choose to continue to make the same choices and move in the same direction as we have always done, or to make significant steps in a new direction.

A person is not poor without a Rupee, but is really poor if without a dream and Ambition. It is not the money, real or imagined, that turns our life around. It is our self confidence that gives us the power to achieve anything and everything including Money that we want. What you think, you actually become.

Trust yourself – A strong positive attitude creates more miracles than anything else, because life is just ten percent how you make it, and ninety percent how you take it.

People always come into your life for a reason, a season or a lifetime.

Not all storms come to disrupt your life, some come to clear your path.

It is good to be independent; all the same, we also need someone who will always be there for us. Love and compassion are necessities, not luxuries. Increase your ability to spread love and happiness. Celebrate life with gratitude.

Remember Success is when you look back at your life and the memories make you smile.

# Chapter 2:

# Human Body

Science and spirituality go hand in hand. You and your body stay together from birth to death and combine uniquely to perform various functions. Once your body system stops, no one is with you. The more you take care of the body, the more the body will take care of you.

Let us commence with a short overview of the basic functioning of the various body systems of our human body before we move to other related aspects.

The subjects in the body broadly are: Organs, Muscles, Skeleton and the Nervous system. The adult human body is made up of hundred trillion cells, two hundred and six bones, six hundred muscles and about seventy-eight organs.

The organ's response to a stimulus is coordinated by the Central Nervous System. The brain stem, at the bottom of the brain, connects the cerebrum with the spinal cord. It includes the mid brain, the pons, and the medulla. It controls the fundamental body functions such as breathing, eye movements, blood pressure, heartbeat, and swallowing.

The organ systems of the body are muscular, skeletal, nervous, circulatory, lymphatic, respiratory, endocrine, immune, urinary/excretory and digestive.

The Skeletal system consists of bones, cartilage, ligaments and tendons. Bones are made up of living tissue consisting of a maximum of calcium and other minerals. As we age, more bone is reabsorbed than is formed resulting in weakness. Red blood cells are formed in the red bone marrow of the bones. The red blood cells carry oxygen around the body allowing energy build up.

The Nervous System consists of the brain, spinal cord, sensory organs, and all of the nerves that connect these organs with the rest of the body. Together, these organs are responsible for the body and the communication among its parts. The nerve cells are very delicate and can repair themselves if damage occurs, except for the cell nuclei. The common disorders of the Nervous System are Depression, Schizophrenia, Multiple Sclerosis, Alzheimer's Disease, Parkinson's Disease and others.

The job of the Circulatory System is to move blood, nutrients, oxygen, carbon dioxide and hormones around the body. It consists of the heart, blood, blood vessels, arteries and veins. The main disorders of heart include Angina Pectoris, Cholesterol, High Blood Pressure, Atherosclerosis, Infarcts and Strokes.

The Digestive System consists of a series of connected organs, that together allow the body to break down and absorb food and remove waste. It includes the mouth, esophagus, stomach, small intestine, large intestine, rectum and anus. The liver and pancreas also play a role in the digestive system because they produce digestive juices. The common digestive disorders are Constipation, Indigestion, Irritable Bowel Syndrome, Gall Stones, Ulcers and Hernia.

The Endocrine System consists of major glands that secrete hormones to the blood. These hormones in turn, travel to different tissues and regulate various bodily functions such as metabolism, growth and sexual function. This system serves as a regulator and helps in integration of the cellular functions and organs. The main glands are Pineal, Pituitary, Thyroid, Adrenal and Pancreas.

The Immune System is the body's defence against bacteria, viruses and other pathogens that may be harmful. It includes lymph nodes, spleen, bone marrow, lymphocytes, thymus and leukocytes which are white blood cells. With age, the thymus begins to shrink and loses its function. The body loses resistance and becomes vulnerable to infections and other diseases.

The Lymphatic System is a drainage system for circulation, which plays an important role in immunity as well as absorption of fats from the intestines, includes lymph nodes, ducts, vessels and plays a role in the body's defence. Its main job is to make and move lymph, a clear fluid that contains White Blood Cells, which help the body fight infection. The lymph nodes are in the neck, armpits, elbows, groins and back of knees and a main one in the chest.

 The Muscular System is responsible for the movement of the human body. It includes joint stability, posture, circulation, respiration, digestion, urination and child birth.

The purpose of the excretory system is to eliminate waste, regulate blood volume and blood pressure, controls levels of electrolytes, metabolites and regulates blood pH (acidity level).

The function of Reproductive System is the fertilization of the female ovum by the male sperm to ensure survival of the species. Human beings propagate the species through sexual reproduction. Humans have a high degree of sexual differentiation.

The Respiratory System consists of the airways, lungs and muscles of respiration responsible for taking in oxygen and expelling carbon dioxide by way of inhalation and exhalation. Oxygen is carried via the lungs to the bloodstream into the cells where energy is released, increasing the cells' ability to function. As we age our lungs lose some of their elasticity, gradually impairing breathing and making the lungs vulnerable to bacterial build up and chest infections.

Stem cells divide to make more stem cells of the same type as a self-renewal process.

The connection between our body, mind and emotions impacts our immune system. Every cell must vibrate at its highest frequency.

Our body is a very complex being, carefully crafted by the master creator and various schools of thought explain its working differently.

As per Ayurveda, the physical body is composed of five elements, namely Earth, Water, Fire, Air and Space. Health consists of a balanced state of three humors (Doshas), seven tissues (Dhatus), three wastes (Malas), and the gastric fire (Agni), together with the balance of the senses, mind and spirit. The Doshas are Vata, Pitta and Kapha.

The said Dhatus consist of:

Rasa (Plasma or Cytoplasm) which contains nutrients from digested food and nourishes all tissues, organs and systems.

Rakta (Blood) governs oxygenation and maintains life function.

Meda (Fat) maintains lubrication of the tissues and protects the body's heat.

Asti (Bone & Cartilage) gives support to body structure.

Majja (Bone marrow and Nerves) fills up the bony spaces, carries motor and sensory impulses, facilities communication among body's cells and organs.

Shukra and Artava (Male and Female reproductive tissues) contain pure essence of all bodily tissues and can create a new life.

Each Dhatu is dependent on previous one. All seven must develop and function properly. The three wastes (Malas) are feces, urine, and sweat which should be produced in adequate amount and get eliminated effectively.

Agni is the heat that governs metabolism and destroys toxins. It sustains life and vitality.

In addition to these bodily factors, the senses, mind and spirit also play a vital role in maintaining good health to produce a state of total happiness.

Anatomic therapy as propounded by Healer Bhaskar states that disease is only in the blood and not in the organs. All the organs are dependent on the quality of blood and required minerals in it.

A general overview of functioning of parts is essential to proceed. Our bodies consist of a number of biological systems that carry out specific functions necessary for everyday living.

Consider your body as a Temple of God. Feel it your duty to keep it fit and fine by observing and obeying the necessary laws of nature.

An understanding of anatomy is key to the practice of medicine and other areas of health.

Everyone must carefully introspect to check whether this sacred gift called the body is being properly used or being misused and mishandled. Your body is either your asset or your liability. Be fit always.

# Chapter 3:

# Human Brain, Mind, Soul, Knowledge, Intelligence

The terms human brain, mind, soul, knowledge and intelligence are closely related; and often used interchangeably; though such interchangeable usage may not always be accurate. Traditionally scientists have tried to define the mind as the product of brain activity. The brain is the physical substance, and the mind is the conscious product of those firing neurons. The Mind goes beyond the physical workings of the brain.

*****

## The Brain and The Mind

Most business is carried out within the space between our two ears. The human mind is a set of cognitive faculties including consciousness, imagination, perception, thinking, judgment, language and memory, which is housed in the brain. It is usually defined as the faculty of an entity's thoughts and consciousness.

The brain works like a complex super-computer. It consists of billions of neurons, each connected to several thousand other neurons. It processes information that it receives from the senses and body and sends messages back to the body. It can also think, and experience emotion, and is the root of human intelligence.

We don't live in our houses – we actually live in our minds. The mind is our permanent residence. It is a vast space with unlimited area. If we keep things messy there, with regrets piled in a corner, expectations stuffed in a closet, secrets and worries under the carpet, comparisons spilt on the table, unwanted worry will attract negativity and drain the physical, mental and spiritual resources at one's disposal. In life, all occurrences are experienced first in the mental frame and then in reality. Your ideas are the most powerful things you have to achieve your aims. Don't choose unhappy thoughts to pervade the conscious mind.

*A Man's life is what his thoughts make of it.*

*- Marcus Aurelius*

The kingdom of happiness is in your thought and feeling. The sub conscious mind can read others thoughts, understand their motives and develop own intuition. Each thought has a frequency, which your sub conscious mind transmits to the universe. The moment you think of something passionately and repeatedly, the law of nature begins to work. When it becomes repeated, intense with emotional appeal, the whole universe gets aligned to help you and this is soon manifested in the real world. You can draw out the hidden powers and wisdom necessary to find joy.

Your sub conscious mind works by intuition and stores your emotions and memories. The conscious and sub conscious mind are at harmony while in sleep. Feed yourself thoughts of desires and goals just before going to bed.

When the mind is weak, a situation is viewed as a problem. When the mind is balanced, the situation is viewed as a challenge. When mind is strong, the situation becomes an opportunity.

Plant the garden of your mind with the seeds of things you want to see grow. Co-create your aims and objectives with the universe.

Our minds are designed to dwell at higher levels. If we want to fly, we have to give up the stuff that weighs us down. Our luggage from the past, our perceptions, our prejudices make up the heavy load that prevents us from rising. Do not let earlier unfavourable experiences or thoughts bog you down. We are born to fly, so stay light.

Always give the mind some positive thoughts to think of and experience those to nullify the influence of life's different situations.

Our Brain works at four basic frequencies. These are Beta, Alpha, Theta and Delta. Beta waves are produced when one is thinking and using one's higher faculties whereas Delta waves are associated with sleep or deep trance like states. The radiant light and flicker rates of television produce Alpha and Theta, essentially a dream like state of mind where the higher critical functions are turned off. The critical side of our brain is the left side, the center of logical human communication and analysis. There are three things the human brain cannot resist noticing – food, attractive people and danger. A human brain has a capacity to store five times as much information as Wikipedia – and by the way, our brain uses the same amount of power as a 10-watt light bulb.

There is very little object of enjoyment in physical aspects of world. It is actually all in the mind. Our mind can be trained. Joys, suffering, tensions all originate in the mind. In fact, we live in the mind and with the mind, all the time all through our life. Your Mind may confuse you but your instinct and intuition will always lead to clarity.

***

# The Soul

We are truly not this body but the spiritual energy that uses the body, energy which is immortal, eternal.

The Soul is the incorporeal essence of a living being, a subtle body. The human spirit includes our intellect, emotions, fears, passions and creativity. Psychologists have concluded that because we cannot directly observe the mind, we should rather study behaviors which are objective manifestations of the mind. Subjects in the mind are psychology, emotions, instincts, personality, individuality, intelligence and memory. Every soul is endowed with minute freedom to choose its priorities. As a point of interest, now neuroscientists use Functional Magnetic Resonance Imaging (fMRIs) to study the brain activities by detecting changes associated with blood flow. They can see parts of the brain light up as the subject processes information. It's a very interesting and emerging study.

The Soul is the Passenger, Intelligence is the Charioteer, Mind is the rope with five horses being the eyes, ears, nose, tongue and skin. The Mind is the master of the senses. If the mind is stronger than intelligence, it will take you in just the opposite direction. Develop your intelligence by reading good books, good association, making the right decisions and avoiding procrastination.

The Soul is permanent and cannot be killed, so do not fear. Develop your soul with strong sense of purpose, connection with source and love with service. The aim is to evolve from lower to higher consciousness, else one might as well have been born an animal and died as one without achieving anything.

Be such a beautiful soul, that people crave for your vibes. Walk away from things that poison your soul; and the happier your life will be.

The main enemies that live inside us are anger, pride, greed and hate. Avoid all of them and have a peaceful life. Beautiful thoughts build a beautiful soul.

Strengthen your Aura by good diet, exercise, good sleep, personal hygiene, positive thoughts and habits.

***

## Knowledge and Wisdom

*Knowledge may be said to be a familiarity, an awareness, or an understanding of someone or something; such as facts (descriptive knowledge), skills (procedural knowledge), or objects (acquaintance knowledge). Knowledge is often described as a belief that is true and justified. This definition has led to its measurement by methods that rely solely on the correctness of answers. Knowledge can be acquired in many different ways and from many sources, including but not limited to perception, reason, memory, testimony, scientific inquiry, education and practice. Knowledge has power and it controls access to opportunity and advancement.*

*Peter Drucker*

Knowledge is knowing that a tomato is a fruit. Wisdom is not putting it in a fruit salad.

Wisdom is the quality of having experience, knowledge and good judgment based on sensible thinking. Again, for instance: A smart person knows what to say but a wise person knows whether to say it or not.

***

# Intelligence

It is the ability to acquire and apply knowledge and skills. Intelligence has been defined in many ways: the capacity for logic, understanding, self-awareness, learning, emotional knowledge, reasoning, planning, creativity, critical thinking and problem solving.

According to Psychologists there are four measures of intelligence:

**Intelligence Quotient (IQ):** This is the measure of the comprehension ability, problem solving such as in mathematics, memory and recall of subject matters, and processing of information, as in logical thinking. It represents largely, academic proficiency.

**Emotional Quotient (EQ):** This is the measure of one's ability to maintain harmony with others, keep to time, be responsible, be honest, respect boundaries, have empathy, which is the ability to share someone else's feelings or experiences by imagining what it would be like to be in that person's situation, be humble, genuine and considerate. It represents one's character.

**Social Quotient (SQ):** This the measure of one's ability to build a network of people and maintain it over a long period of time. It represents your charisma.

**Adversary Quotient (AQ):** This refers to the measure of one's ability to go through a rough patch in life and come through without losing one's mind. It determines who will give up in the face of troubles to the extent that they may desert their own families and mentors.

Psychologists use the word temperament to describe the emotional aspect that reflects one's personality.

**Type A** personalities, by their nature, strive for personal recognition, are aggressive, hasty, impatient, explosive and loud in speech; while **Type B** personalities are more laid back, even tempered, patient and with a relaxed attitude.

Intelligence may also be classified as below:

**Linguistic:** Language skills, oratory and reading.

**Logical:** Mathematical / Logical intelligence.

**Music:** Helps you to keep rhythm and create music characteristics.

**Visual / Spatial:** This is associated with artistic ability such as abilities of painters, sculptors, interior designers and engineers.

**Physical**: It includes athletic ability and body movement as well as skills required by carpenters, surgeons and others. It is also called Kinesthetic Intelligence.

**Interpersonal**: Ability to be good and make people comfortable around you such as Teachers, Managers, Motivational speakers.

**Intrapersonal**: The capacity of self-analysis and the ability to examine one's own behavior, day dreaming, accessing one's own intuitive nature.

Knowledge is infinite. Knowledge without intelligence makes us indecisive. Intelligence without knowledge makes us short sighted. Strength without intelligence makes us dumb tools at the hands of others. Intelligence without strength cannot realize dreams.

***

# Memory

Memory is made up of neural traces created in the brain. These chemical links are created by several kinds of action, the most common being an initial sensory or emotional event, and sustained repetition of that event.

Registration occurs when something comes to your attention or has meaning for you. If you want to remember an OTP long enough to punch it, then you won't go any further, but if you want to use your ATM pin, then you have to do more to instill it as a permanent memory. Retention occurs when the aim is to hold the information for a long time. Recall is crucial to access the stored information.

As you age, memory may lose its sharpness or acuity, in a random manner. Keep notes for ready references.

Science has focused on the material aspects, assuming that stimuli and responses are suggestive of thought and emotion. Reality is seen in what we do, more than in what we think. Measurement limits science; be it an intelligence quotient or emotional index while there is much more to it than modern science can reach out to.

*****

# Chapter 4:

# The Stages Of Aging In Life

Ageing is commonly taken to mean advancement in years with time. Growing old is universal and inevitable in our life.

*The two most important days in your life are the day you are born, and the day you find out why.*

*Mark Twain*

There are three types of ages in human beings chronological, biological and psychological.

The Chronological Age is counted by the number of calendar years beginning from birth and is numerically fixed. It is convenient for counting and universally accepted, though not always a reliable indicator.

The Biological indicator is considered in terms of critical life signs and cellular processes. The appearance and functioning of the body can change by good diet, exercise, life style. So biologically the body can look younger or older depending on how you treat it.

The Psychological Age is more flexible and personal. Mental agony brought by depression, mental stress, grief, worry; and ailments, such as high blood pressure, heart disease and diabetes can adversely affect the body, and therefore how old it actually appears to be or behaves.

An optimistic outlook, jovial behavior and happy moods must be induced.

Other factors that contribute to ageing are genes, chemical reactions within the body, and reduction in the efficiency of brain, endocrine and immune systems due to the natural process of ageing.

*****

# Arrival of The Soul

Destiny determines our family, body, our social set up. It is later, that our desires may accept or reject it. It is not clear when the soul actually enters the womb, whether on conception or sometime later. It is believed that a soul chooses its family, life, success, setbacks and its departure mode but is consciously unaware of it.

Physically we get born out of the mother's womb into human culture but it is the day when you come out of your ignorance, awakening arises and you are aware of your infinite nature that you can say you are truly born or reborn.

We cannot enter this world and expect to find everything just the way we would like it or want it to be. There are disappointments and unexpected happenings, but despite all upheavals we can carry ourselves safely and with poise.

We were never created to live depressed, guilty, condemned, ashamed or unworthy lives; but to be victorious and happy.

*****

# Infancy

Childbirth is the start of the life cycle journey. Infants differ in size, physiological features, physical proportions, physiological functions and appearance. Growth and development occur by intake of oxygen, milk or equivalent, other appropriate nutrition and elimination of waste products. The other basic needs are sleep, rest and activity. This period extends to about two weeks after birth. Children are born with characteristic temperamental differences as seen in their activity rate and sensitivities from which their personality pattern will develop.

Mystery surrounds the transmigration of souls and how we actually acquire a new life form and choose our families to get born into. But nonetheless, we have arrived on the scene and survival begins.

Everyone is born with some unique talent capable of being nourished and attaining its true potential. Look deeper within yourself and identify, you will find more than one.

***

# Babyhood

This period extends from infancy to about two years. The baby develops motor skills including the use of limbs and play skills. Common emotional patterns are joy, anger and fear of stimuli. The baby learns to pronounce words partly by trial and error, but mainly by imitating adult speech which starts to clear by about eighteen months. The first attempt is one word followed by a gesture. The first social smile appears at around 6 weeks of age. The core of personality development, consisting of self-concept remains fundamentally the same as far as the personality development is concerned. Cultural differences exist among many forms of child discipline.

***

# Early Childhood

Childhood is the age span from about two years to adolescence. Childhood is the time for children to be in school and at play, to grow strong and confident with the love and encouragement of family. It is a precious time, in which children should live safely and be protected from abuse and exploitation by others. It consists of early childhood from two years to six years and late childhood from six years to the adolescent stage.

Learning gives creativity. Creativity leads to thinking.

Academics is an important part of their curriculum as their future life will largely depend upon that. Today's modern education system is based on more of knowledge from books and less from understanding of life. Today many students have an abundance of knowledge but the wisdom of life is largely missing.

***

# Adolescence

Adolescence is the period of transition between childhood and adulthood. It includes major changes to the body and is the period of life in which the way a young person relates to the world is determined. Physical, sexual, cognitive, social and emotional changes that happen during this time may bring both, a sense of anticipation, as well as anxiety for children and their families. Understanding what to expect at different stages promotes healthy development. There may be a generation gap felt between adolescents and their parents.

## Early Adolescence

During this stage children often start to grow more quickly. They also begin to notice other body changes. These body changes can inspire curiosity and anxiety especially if they do not know what to expect or what is normal.  Early adolescents have concrete black and white thinking without much room in between. Flexible thinking is like being ready to duck and weave, dodge and flow. If you are flexible as you grow, you will have a happy future.

## Middle Adolescence

Physical changes continue during middle adolescence. Adolescents may experience voice cracking and acne. At this stage many teens become interested in romantic relationships. Many middle adolescents have more arguments with their parents as they struggle for more independence; peer pressure may peak at this age. They are very concerned about their appearance. The brain continues to change and mature during this stage, but there are still many differences in how a normal middle adolescent thinks, when compared to an adult.

The Frontal lobe plays a major role in coordinating, complex decision making, impulse control and being able to control multiple options and consequences. While they may be able to walk through the logic of avoiding risks outside these situations, strong emotions often continue to drive their decisions; and impulses come into play, rather than logic and common sense. It is better for them to collect their wits, allow themselves to calm down and then find an appropriate response.

## Late Adolescence

They have generally completed physical development and grown to their full adult height. They usually, though not necessarily, have more impulse control and may be better able to gauge risks and rewards. Teens entering early adulthood have a strong sense of their own individuality now, and can identify their own values. They become more emotionally and physically separated from the family.

Life's challenges should not paralyze you but help in discovering who you are. The value system that has been inculcated, either stands implemented, or discarded almost entirely at times. Once the thinking gets crystallized, rigid and formed one will find it difficult to navigate back. If, at this stage, you think you have all the answers you are sadly mistaken. The older you get, there will be more areas to experience without guidelines. We first make our habits, then our habits make us.

Do not try and control the lives of others. Learn to manage your own affairs and make yourself and your parents proud of your positive achievements. Never be a home breaker and never judge your parents. You have no idea what their life has been, focus on yours and be a good human being.

***

# Adulthood

An adult is a person who has attained the age of maturity as specified by law, in other words also fully grown or developed.

The main developmental tasks of adulthood are getting started in an occupation, selecting a mate, starting a family, rearing kids, managing a home, finding a congenial social group. Nobody owes it to you, you owe it to yourself. You should have a strong understanding of who you are.

Every action you take, every decision you make, everything you do has an immediate effect on those around you – and on you. Your actions will dictate in general, whether your life is going to run happily or badly, smoothly or as if wheels have fallen off.

If you are selfish and manipulative it will rebound on you. Whatever you do and how you do it, will come back to you in spades. What goes around, comes around. Do the right thing always. Never take undue advantage of someone else's low point in life.

Early adulthood, middle adulthood and late adulthood are three main stages of physical, emotional and psychological development.

They are characterized by maturity, self-confidence, autonomy, decision making, and are generally more practical, self-directed, experienced and less open minded and receptive to change. All these traits affect their motivation as well as their ability to learn.

Youthfulness is the biggest treasure you have. Have clear goals. Learn from failures. Overcome your guilt and worry. Develop the right sense of loyalty. By constantly rising and adjusting one's life intentions, actions and environment more fully to the mode of goodness, one will gradually rise up to the platform of achieving a naturally healthy, enjoyable, blissful, knowledgeable and successful life.

Where do you stand?

***

# Association

Explaining the meaning of Association: "A rain drop from the sky: if caught by clean hands, is pure enough for drinking. If it falls in the gutter, its value falls so much that it can't be used for washing even your feet. If it falls on a hot surface, it will evaporate. If it falls on a lotus leaf, it shines like a pearl. The drop is the same but its existence and worth depends on whom it is associated with."

The ability to discern is about the ability to discriminate the right from the wrong and truth from false.

Always be associated with people who are good natured, not mean, selfish or back stabbing. You cannot change the people around you, but you can change the people that you choose to be around and you will experience your inner transformation.

Be picky about who you keep around you. Personalities, words and traits do rub off naturally.

You are the books you read, the movies you watch, the music you listen and people you spend time with, the conversations you engage in. Choose wisely what you feed your mind. Prevention is always better than cure.

***

# Finding A Partner

Finding a rich person as your partner is not your fortune, but finding a life partner who cares about you, respects you, takes care of your self-respect and is honest with you and vice versa can surely make your life fortunate.

The best and the most beautiful things in this world cannot be seen or heard, but must be felt with the heart. Life without love is like a tree without flowers. It is better to have loved and lost than never to have loved at all.

Online sites are convenient for match making but you need to exercise caution and discretion. Sometimes good people make bad choices. It doesn't mean they are bad people. It means they are human.

It is never too late to fall in love.

Your spouse could be your Wife or Husband or Live-In Partner. When you find someone, who makes you feel the same way music does, that's when you have found your someone special.

***

# House

A house may be self-acquired or inherited. It everyone's dream to have at least one house in a life time in keeping with ones likes and preferences. Loans are the common remedy, but you end up paying a lot more than you borrow; but there is no easy route for the middle class.

It would be good to research about Geopathic stress before to proceed to buy a property. The Earth resonates at about a frequency falling in range of alpha human brainwaves. Underground streams, sewers, water pipes, electricity, tunnels, mineral formations and geological faults distort the natural resonance of the earth thus creating geopathic stress. Sleeping or spending a lot of time in geopathic stress zones can have an ill effect on our health, performance and wellbeing. Vastu Study is very commonly followed as a science of Architecture, originated in India.

It is better to invest in house even if you have an ancestral one, as the future is unpredictable and your own little home by your hard work gives you infinite joy.

*** 

# Mid Life Crisis

In this time of life, between forty years and sixty years of age, people experience many physical changes that signal the person is aging, including grey hair and hair loss, wrinkles and age spots, problems with vision, hearing loss, weight gain – commonly called the middle age spread – and also the onset of memory loss. Men undergo a change in virility and women find a change in fertility. This transition requires new adjustments.

This is also often described as an age of stress. Somatic stress is there due to physical evidences of ageing. Economic stress results from financial burden of educating children. Psychological stress may be a result of the death of a spouse, separation, boredom and neglect. Sometimes these factors bring about stagnation in professional and personal relationships.

Know about Elder Neglect and financial exploitation where their abusers are often adult children or even younger spouses. It could be in the form of physical, mental abuse, isolating, ignoring, intimidation with threats, inappropriate medication, confinement and financial trickery. Speak up, everyone deserves to live in safety with dignity and respect. Know the laws that protect you.

To keep up a good level of optimism and passion for life, keep setting higher goals and add more value to your lives.

 People often take a break from worldly responsibilities to reflect upon the deeper meaning of their lives with new understanding.

***

## Mature Adulthood

Life undergoes changes both physical and mental with age. Ageing is a universal genetic process. Anticipate the change, express your feelings to your family members, maintain a good support network, keep good health by balanced diet, physical and mental exercises.

Bring back control into your life, avoid attachment, reassess priorities and maintain an optimistic outlook. Devise an action plan for the future, of personal wellbeing, support network and routine for keeping yourself occupied.

Avoid stress and anxiety, as they produce stress hormones increasing cholesterol, triglycerides, arthritis, fatty liver, along with many other imbalances.

These people have usually raised families, established themselves in their work life, contributed, having acquired a rich repository of experiences, with which they can help to guide others' reservoirs of wisdom. They represent the source of wisdom that exists in each one of us, helping us to avoid the mistakes of the past, while reaping the benefits of life's lessons.

Homes for the aged may also be viable options for those who have been deserted, or are lonely, dejected, suffering ill health, and in conflict with opportunistic members of the household.

Prepare your Will and Settlements with a copy held with your Attorney / Executor.

Prepare your mind for old age. Be content with your productive life: Tell yourself "I am content with my achievement." You played your best innings, now you wish to enjoy these moments in peace. Learn the art of ageing gracefully and spiritually.

Your old age should be like a Banyan tree, as it becomes old it bends, bows towards the soil only to support the next branches of trees. You will get lots of happiness, goodness and positivity when you give back to the system.

When you feel lonely, get ready and go out to a public park, or read, meditate, sleep, or follow your hobbies, talk to your partner or well-wisher. Avoid brooding and constant thoughts of despair. Always remain cheerful.

*Until death comes, all is life*

*- Ruskin Bond*

# Good Bye

The difference between being alive or dead is one of a mere single additional breath. This grim reality hits one when somebody known passes away. When and how it will happen is unknown; but that it will happen at any time is a certainty. We should remember it more often. It will put life in perspective.

Remain humble even if you reach the farthest part of the sky. No matter how far you go, in the end you too will be laid into the soil, shed the false sense of prestige, riches and superiority.

This thought will help you remain rooted to the ground, be humble and compassionate. Thinking of the impermanence of life will make you less selfish and help in becoming better human being. Remember, unto dust thou art born, unto dust thou shall return.

If you have ever been to a graveyard / cemetery you would recollect the immense sense of calm and practical feeling of being grounded.

Most human beings approach their graves with their talent unused. Those in our lives who are dying and have died, teach us about the value of living. They remind us not to take our lives for granted, but to live each moment of life to its fullest, and to remember that our own small lives form a part of the greater whole. Did we even take note of it?

Death means the soul leaves the body and has a new body ready for it to use and carries with it, its baggage of Karma.

One morning a wealthy man sat on his balcony enjoying sunshine and his coffee when a little ant caught his eye; it was trying to carry a big leaf several times its size. In front of his eyes there was this tiny creature of God, lacking in size yet equipped with a brain to analyze, contemplate, reason, explore, discover and overcome. A while later the man saw the creature had reached its destination – a tiny hole in the floor which was the entrance to its underground dwelling. And it was at that point that ant's shortcoming in common with the Man was revealed. How could the ant carry into the tiny hole, the large leaf that it had carefully managed to bring close to the destination? It simply couldn't! It had to leave it behind and went home empty handed. The ant had not thought about the end before it began its challenging journey; and in the end, the large leaf had been nothing more than a burden to it. The creature had no option but to leave it behind to reach its destination. The man had learnt a great lesson that day. That is the truth about our lives too.

We worry about our families, we worry about our jobs, we worry about how to earn more money, we worry about where we should live, what kind of vehicle to buy, what kind of dress to wear, what gadgets to upgrade, only to abandon all these things, when we reach our destination – we don't realize in our lives' journeys that these are just burdens that we are carrying with utmost care and fear of losing them; only to find at the end they are useless and we can't take them with us. Don't have regrets and remorse.

A sick man turned to his doctor, as he was preparing to leave the examination room and said, "Doctor I am afraid to die. Tell me what lies on the other side."

The doctor was holding the handle of the door, on the other side came a sound of scratching and whining; as he opened the door, a dog sprang into the room and leaped on him with an eager show of gladness.

Turning to the patient the doctor said, "Did you notice my dog? He has never been in this room before. He didn't know what was inside. He knew nothing except that his master was here, and when the door opened, he sprang in without fear. I know little of what is on the other side of death – but I know one thing that my master is there – call him what you may."

The Divine transcends all human understanding.

Settle your conflicts as much as is feasible. Give wisdom and share experience with others. Put something back. Check how many trees you planted. How many children's education you have sponsored, how much pro bono work you have done, the list can be endless.

Make arrangements for your settlements and dues. Wish what you would like your next life to be. What would you like your tomb stone to read? Check what history will say about you and what would your cosmic record read like.

Do not be paranoid about leaving the world when your time comes naturally. Be at peace and leave without regret. Everything that you love, you will eventually lose; but in the end, love will return in a different form.

***

# Chapter 5:
# *Stages Of Standard Working/ Professional Life*

## Student / Education

Every student has a dream to succeed in life, but not all are fortunate enough to get the right type of family, guidance and tools to achieve their desired goals. The foundation stone of a successful life is laid down during student years.

Classroom learning is the first part of school going. What is more important is your self-study, research, practical understanding of concepts and to be able to put them into perspective.

Preparation before class and quick recapitulation after class must be followed. Retain and recall and do systematic revision. Solving old question papers is a time-tested method. Preparation just before exam must be more focused.

Studying late night versus early morning study have their respective advantages and disadvantages. Use the schedule format that works best for you and alternate whenever needed.

Overcome fear, stress, distractions, low self-esteem, low will power and poor concentration.

Do physical and mental exercises to improve your concentration. A workout followed by breathing exercises, followed by meditation or Yoga, if practiced correctly, can be very useful. Use visualization techniques for positive affirmations. Music can make you feel good and rejuvenated. Play your favorite tunes often.

Presentation skills in exams clearly provide a leading edge and help in surging ahead.

Never decrease the goal – rather increase the effort to achieve it. Taking on the challenge of expanding our comfort zone brings us out of ourselves and keeps us learning and growing. The infinite sky is the limit.

Mind mapping is a way of linking key concepts using images, lines and links. It uses the concept of radiant thinking which is thoughts radiating out from a single idea, often expressed as an image. It is a visual tool to help structure information and reflects how the brain actually works. It allows you to represent a tremendous amount of information in a relatively small space. It can be used for many purposes like note making, brain storming, problem solving, memorization, planning and presentation. Read smarter, not typically harder, and understand the difference.

Refine your memory by sensory associations, coding the points, making a rhyme. Read out loud. Enjoy the process of learning and remembering, practice as actuals, make flash cards, mind maps. Revise before you sleep and find it easy to recall in the morning.

Concentration is the ability to work intensely at a task, to the exclusion of every other demand on your attention. Avoid external distractions such as noise, environment; and internal ones such as poor diet, lack of exercise or inadequate sleep.

If concentration is monitored pro-actively, it could give an indication of one's area of excellence. This could be done by homing in on one's aptitudes, just as an activity in which one completely loses awareness of time and space.

Smart work is the secret to success. Start with finding a suitable study place and make it a comfort zone. Post a lot of positive messages around the space. Define your goals and objectives. Without goals that are clearly defined, articulated and written, you will drift away in life.

Challenge yourself, set priorities and be specific. Expect failure, revisit, link your goals and re start.

Look for your core talent and bring it out, do not forget to express gratitude to your mentors, even if you fall out with them.

As far as specialized subjects are concerned Ethics, Law, Vocational Training, Robotics and Coding needs to be to better incorporated. We need a more value-based education. The educational curriculum must include teaching the rules of cause and effect and to be self-reliant.

A morally educated and rule abiding person would be much better equipped to adapt and be well adjusted than a morally bankrupt and lawless person with only high academic qualifications to his credit.

Time Management is crucial. Make a schedule, start to follow it as your study periods. Make extensive use of flash cards in idle time and during waiting periods. Identify and make best use of your alertness cycles. Keep consolidating and moving ahead.

*Education is not the learning of facts but training the mind to think.*

*- Albert Einstein*

The brain is like a super computer, learn to make best use of it. Success, failure and mediocrity are all habits; what would you want for yourself?

Go beyond the techniques and strategies given in books. Give your imagination wings to fly.

Direction is so much more important than speed. Some are going fast nowhere. It is convenient to just look up the internet and find the first possible notes given and conclude your project work; but is that all? Learn to work more diligently and develop all your mental faculties.

Focus on concentration of power. Create a vision, follow role models and achievable goals. Most effective people concentrate on their areas of excellence.

If you have an idea, execute it. If you have knowledge, give it out. If you have a goal, achieve it. Don't wait to start.

Elite education has its own serious drawbacks. Develop a broader vision. Never think you know everything, or that whatever you have studied is the only thing that constitutes complete knowledge. Be open minded.

We certainly don't need learned monsters, skilled psychopaths, educated illiterates. Teachers must help students become more humane and service oriented.

*Hard work beats talent when talent doesn't work hard*

*- Tim Notke*

***

# Career

You have to think of your future anyway, so why not think big! Make your ideal path – it doesn't come by just waiting for it. A clear plan takes away the burden of choice.

Career is an occupation undertaken for a significant period of a person's life and with opportunities for progress. Everyone must engage in some outward actions in the material world to earn his living.

Success introduces you to the world. Failure is often the stepping stone to success. Increase your value. Search for different ways in which you can accomplish your goals. Focus on soft skills after acquiring your technical expertise.

Generally, there are five career stages which an individual has to undergo during his life time. Exploration is the pre-employment stage, wherein the individuals are in their mid-twenties and enter the work environment from college life.

Take the whole responsibility on your shoulders and know that you are the creator of your own destiny. All the strength and succor you want is within yourself. Stop blame games and lame excuses.

Where you start is not as important as where you finish.

***

# Job Search

Belief, faith and conviction are words that move mountains. Endeavor to begin well.

Post out your Resume displaying the confidence you have in yourself and your major achievements.

Dress smartly and make a lasting first impression. Develop good mannerisms. Market yourself well.

Whatever you decide to do, make sure it makes you truly happy and put your heart and soul into your work. Your dream job does not exist, you have to create it.

Make the best use of online job application systems and online screenings.

The qualification that gave you a job, is the same qualification someone else also had but did not bag the job. Be grateful and humble.

***

# Intern Establishment

This is where the Individual actually experiences work culture. All expectations and fantasies come to an end and one has to face the reality of life. Intelligence is quickness to learn, and this is a key attribute. Competence is ability with willingness and desire to apply what is learned; desire is the attitude which makes a skillful person competent. Many skilled people can remain incompetent.

This is also called the learning stage. Choose the profession that you like. Alternatively, you can do business or work related to your dream idea. This is the stage where you have clearly decided to follow your chosen path of profession and need to go all guns blazing.

Kind words to interns at work can be short and easy to speak, but their echoes are truly endless.

Establishment is where the Individual actually experiences work culture. It is also part of the learning stage. Even if you are on the right track, you will get run over if you just sit there and while away your time especially by over indulgence in mobile entertainment.

Each person must live by the earnings made through his or her own mental or physical labor.

***

# Mid-Career

This generally covers the period between the ages of thirty-five to forty-five years. Here one must evaluate one's current position whether one is advancing, stabilized or declining. One has to also maintain balance between career and personal life. There is a desire to expand one's influence and commitment to family, society and future generations.

***

# Late Career

An individual reaches to a particular position in the organizational hierarchy on the basis of his career graph which is characterized by growth or stagnation. One can mentor and guide others through real time experiences. Being a Mentor puts one in a position of greater power and responsibilities. One can bring about positive organizational changes.

***

# Build Your Own Business

Starting your own business requires greater hard work, dedication and perseverance. Hard work puts you where good luck can find you.

When a business starts with minimal investment, the enterprise must focus on generating cash from the outset by building a paying customer base quickly.

Focus your skill entirely around what you can do best. To create a working system that allows you to focus, you must create time by limiting sheer volume of different things to be done, essentially by outsourcing.

Good ideas are everywhere, look for them. Focus on risks that may cause potential failure. Be optimistic as well as realistic.

Play to your strengths and become an expert in your chosen field. Strive for excellence.

Be conversant with local labor laws and the market system. Research well before you start. It is essential.

*A businessman was once in debt and could not see a way out. Creditors and suppliers were demanding payments. He sat in the park, deep in thought, wondering if anything could save his company from bankruptcy. Suddenly an old man appeared before him and said, "I can see something is troubling you." After* *listening patiently, the old man said I believe that I can help you. He asked the Man his name, wrote out a cheque and put it into his hands saying, "Take this money, meet me here exactly one year later and you can pay me back at that time." Then he turned and disappeared as he had come. The business man saw in his hands a cheque for $ 500,000 signed by Warren Buffet, one of the world's richest men. "I can erase my worries instantly," he realized. But instead, the man decided to put the uncashed cheque in his safe, knowing that it might give him the strength to work out how to save his business and to use this only in case of dire emergency. With changed thinking he negotiated better deals, restructured his business and worked vigorously with zeal and enthusiasm and got several big contracts. Within a few months, he was out of debt and started making money once again. Exactly one year later, he returned to the park with the uncashed cheque. As agreed, the old man appeared. But just as the business man was about to hand him back the cheque and share his success story, a nurse came running up and grabbed the old man. "I am so glad I caught him," she cried. "I hope he hasn't been bothering you much. He always escapes from the mental hospital and tells people that he is Warren Buffet!" Saying this she took the old man away. The surprised man stood there just stunned! All year long he had been dealing in business thinking that he had half a million dollars behind him!*

Life's greatest setbacks reveal biggest opportunities.

Success and riches are not for the weak. Don't lose your energy when you suffer setbacks on your road to success, keep removing the hurdles and keep marching ahead.

***

# Target, Deadlines, Resources

Phases are temporary, cycles are eternal. A problem is a chance for you to do your best. The beginning is always the hardest, don't think of giving up.

If your job is not your passion, make it your passion, bring in innovations. A job done better than anticipated and before the time allocated is the best form of result.

Efficiency is how well you can manage your time with your priorities and yet make it look so simple! Focus and concentration will allow you to complete your task in time and avoid derailments.

Lakhs of people are also suffering from a less than optimal work life balance. Some youngsters wish to achieve everything in life so soon, even going to the extent of looking for unethical short cuts to quick success or money.

You must draw lines and between your work and life. Walk Stand, Run in your lane and be patient. The better you understand the beliefs, actions, desires and wants of others, the more likely you are to make the right response, alter your own thinking where necessary, and generally be successful.

Sometimes you put in loads of effort and get nothing back. You work up a sweat while others cruise along. Well, you have to keep on doing your hundred percent, because you don't know what part of your effort will pay off. Your efforts will get rewarded eventually, but you may not know which ones worked and which didn't. Always be on the lookout for ways to constantly improve yourself.

Those who have learned to collaborate and improvise most effectively have prevailed. Think more in terms of 'We' rather than 'I'.

Only humans think that lack of success in a few attempts is defined as failure, but the truth is that we fail only when we stop trying.

Bad things do happen, how you respond to them defines your real character of strength.

Reinterpret a difficult situation in a more enlightened and empowering way. It can change your life.

Performance is potential minus internal interference.

*****

## Towards Your Boss

As a subordinate, try to understand your Bosses' points of view and to see things from the company's perspective. Know your boundaries. Reflect constantly. Don't be stuck to your way of doing things.

When you cannot control what is happening, challenge yourself to control the way you respond to what is happening.

*We cannot direct the wind, but we can adjust the sails.*

*-Bertha Calloway*

That is where your power lies.

Be a good listener. Listen twice the amount you speak. Resist the temptation to interrupt unnecessarily.

There is a certain kind of valour in being polite. Disagree softly when you must but it must be based on true conviction and justification. Learn to say 'No' gracefully.

You have to nurture your habits. The world is changing in favour of those who command knowledge and understanding more than just routine experience.

*** 

# Towards Your Peers

A good Man makes his life with the bricks that adversity throws at him. Smile always when you meet someone, it breaks the ice.

Some tasks are carried out independently and some in teams. Your peers could be your closest confidants as well as greatest critics. Remember they are also your competitors.

Discuss issues but do not argue. Try walking away rather than arguing.

Don't gossip. People who gossip about others with you will do the same about you in your absence.

Excellence in work brings true recognition. Don't be disappointed when people refuse to help you. Remember the words of *Albert Einstein: I am thankful to all those who said no; because of them I did it myself.*

Be there for others but don't leave yourself behind.

Get good at being uncomfortable and stop walking the path of least resistance. Handle whatever comes by.

When you look for the good in others, you discover the best in yourself.

The one who is constantly flying with zeal and enthusiasm brings progress in others too.

We have the ability to turn our adversaries into our team mates and even our saviors.

Keep the company of people who are dreamers and doers. Surround yourself with believers and thinkers.

You don't have to be perfect to inspire others. Let people get inspired by how you deal with your imperfections.

***

# Towards Your Subordinates

Successful leaders have been quoted as being the best, demonstrating wisdom, motivating the team, giving confidence and credit to their subordinates.

Perhaps the biggest mistake anyone can make is to adopt one style to all disregarding changing situations and circumstances.

Don't analyze the problem from an expert point of view alone. Be practical also.

A problem well stated is a problem half solved. Try it.

Be a role model for junior staff. Encourage them by example. Give them a break, a chance, a bit of slack.

Sympathy is I understand how you feel. Empathy is I feel how you feel. The latter is more important. Listen to feelings and not just words. It conveys much more.

You may stay committed to your decisions, but stay flexible in your approach.

Motivation is the inner condition that energizes and directs us toward purposive goal seeking behavior.

***

# Crisis Management

Everything is difficult before it becomes easy. We must not run away from our problems. Hold on there! If you are facing a tunnel, be sure there is an opening at the end of the road, cross it to feel the new experience.

Learn to adjust. Be yourself. Be adaptable to change. Learn from failures. Identify your aptitude. Focus all your energies. Take course corrections. See what the system expects from you.

Have goals. To be agreeable when we disagree is a goal most of us have to keep working on. Have clear goals and values. Have clarity and conviction in communication.

In general, complaining arrests growth. A person whose mind is wanting to complain, more often is the one who refuses to take the responsibility. Train your mind to discover good from the dump of negativity, learn to turn frustrations into inspiration and keep going on. You will be able to build a reservoir of positive energy and get into a forward progression mode.

Be free form envy and ego. Continuously polish yourself. Don't become a case of born to win, but conditioned to lose. Ability without the right attitude is wasted.

Interpersonal skills are very important in any profession. It is a must possess quality.

Ego is the unhealthy attitude that results in arrogance. Healthy pride is a feeling of the pleasure of accomplishment with humility.

Laugh when you can, apologize when you should and let go of what you can't change. If you haven't tried to learn it at home, you will find it difficult to handle it at your workplace.

Take a step back for a broader perspective. Try to handle situations or events with curiosity and humor, instead of unwanted urgency and misjudged alarm. Devise your unique method.

No one has travelled the road of success without crossing the streets of failure. If you don't step forward you will always remain in the same place.

Listen to inspirational talks, read self-help books, stay in the company of the optimistic.

Involve all stake holders and address their concerns.

***

# Retirement

*A retired MD of a bank came to a branch in his city where nobody recognized him, as the branch was being run by people from the new generation. He had to identify himself as ex MD of the same bank. Curiously one employee of that branch asked him, "How is life after retirement?" The ex-MD said, "I have realized that after the Chess game is over, the king and soldiers are kept in the same box."*

Retirement is not the end of the road. It is the beginning of the open highway.

The meaning of retirement is not to retire from life; professional retirement only suggests that you have retired from a formal, fixed-time work place. A person has to step out of work or get a retirement. It is considered to be one of the most difficult stages.

What feels like the end, is often the beginning if analyzed positively. Find something purposeful to engage with. Plan your finances judiciously.

Retirement age seems a controversial concept, as mostly you retire a person when he is at the peak of his capability. With increase in life expectancy and health standards, this aspect needs to be revisited including age restrictions for applying for Government as well as Private Sector jobs.

***

## Post Retirement

Nobody is ever too old to learn. Always be in transit in life. Never lose your gusto.

While some would like to get re employed due to their family commitments, many would like to start a business, pursue their hobbies or do social work.

Life is short; if there was ever a moment to follow your passion which you could not earlier, and do something that you always wanted to, the moment is Now.

Spend well on yourself and your spouse before others. Beware of people who may eye your life long earnings.

The World does not rest on your shoulders; you don't have to constantly correct people; after all the onus of making everyone perfect is not on you.

Don't be embarrassed by your emotions, after all that's what makes you human.

After loving parents, siblings, spouse, and children; my friends, start loving yourself too, better late than never.

Rewrite the story of your life, be the person you dreamt to be or now want to be. Do not wait till the end, to come to terms with the meaning of life and the precious role you deserve.

You can completely recreate yourself. Nothing is permanent. You are not stuck. You have choices. You can think new thoughts, learn something new, new habits. All that matters is you decide today and don't look back.

Retirement is the only time when in your life when time no longer equals money.

Retire from the job but never retire your mind.

Retirement is when you stop living at work and start working at living. Keep adding value to your lives.

***

# Chapter 6:
# Management Of Relationships

This process of living involves both growth and adjustment. We must adjust in order to survive to maintain a comfortable relation with others and our surroundings.

The relationship between humans is largely governed by desire and action. From desire flows yearning, attachment, greed, pride, jealousy, frustration, rage, source of all problems.

Don't hate yourself. The environment may make you feel guilty of things you never did. The good you find in others is also in you. The faults you find in others are your faults as well. The world around you is a reflection at large.

If one is not happy in a situation with another, one is probably caught in a chronic painful pattern.

Beware of half-truths and misinterpretation of facts. Get advice from the successful and the wise. One's life is a relationship with everything one comes across. Clarity in relationships develops compassion and love.

*To get angry with the right person, to the right degree, at the right time, for the right purpose, and in the right way is not easy.*

*- Aristotle*

Each pain makes you stronger, each betrayal more intelligent, every disappointment more skillful and each experience more wise. Setbacks are inevitable. They act as driving forces and also teach us humility. It is better to learn from the mistakes of others.

None of us know what might happen even the next minute; yet we still go forward as we trust and have faith in most of our relationships. However, loving someone may not always result in similar reciprocation.

When someone lies to you, it teaches you that things are not always as what they seem. The truth is often far beneath the surface. When someone steals your dearest ones it teaches you that nothing is forever.

Avoid 'whataboutery' in all relationships. Those who cannot learn from the past are condemned to repeat it. Be someone's strength, someone's inspiration.

Walk away from arguments that lead you nowhere but anger. Be strong enough to walk away from what isn't the best for you, and be patient enough to wait for the blessings you deserve. Never make permanent decisions on temporary feelings. Success is what happens after you have survived all your disappointments.

The moment you accept responsibility for everything in your life, is when you gain the power to change anything in your life.

There is no perfect life; but we can fill it with perfect moments. Sometimes we don't appreciate what we already have because we are too focused on what we want.

Each word has a frequency, an energy that sends impulses to the brain and we produce chemicals whereby we feel happy or angry, or something else. Feelings are important in our lives as they come from the heart; if we respond, they grow, if we ignore them, they die and if we respect them, they stay forever. Listen with ears of tolerance. See through the eyes of compassion. Speak with the language of love.

The path isn't a straight line, it is a spiral. You continuously come back to things you thought you understood and see deeper truths. Time, health and relationships do not come with price tags. But when we lose them we realize the cost, often too late. So therefore,

@ Before you assume, learn the facts and remove the  bias.

@ Before you judge, understand why and how come.

@ Before you hurt or interfere, feel it yourself.

@ Before you speak, think again.

@ Before you act, be sure of the consequences and guilt.

Perceptions could be very different from reality. Ultimately life should also be more than just solving problems. Hope and end are always there for everyone.

Every phase of our life is bound to teach us something valuable, but it depends on us to take lessons or just turn the page.

Never play mind games, you will always end losing - not the game but the relationship!

***

# Growing Up Relationships

These are very complex and evolving. Often one person is simpler and the other more crooked. No two people are the same. The physically strong dominates the weak. Nature compensates the weak by greater smartness.

Individuals are inclined to conform to peer pressure. Virtue is looking beyond selfish need and agenda and being concerned about others.

The arrival of a new baby also sparks off intense emotions. The young child who has been accustomed to his parents undivided attention may exhibit outbursts of anger and jealously.

Many today, are actually learning their attitudes and values from movies and web series. Soap operas again largely glamourize pre-marital and extramarital sex. Pornography is another threat which de-humanizes men and women; and often showcases criminal sexual activity. Drinking, smoking, drugs are glamourized without realization of the costs in terms of precious lives and livelihood.

Prosperity brings friends and adversity reveals them. We don't make friends anymore; we add them nowadays. People make friendships for either pleasure or convenience and true friendship is becoming rare.

Anything we practice long enough becomes ingrained into our system and becomes a habit. A person's character is the sum total of their habits. If we lie once, it becomes lot easier to do it the second and third time. Habits are a lot stronger than logic and reasoning. If we don't decide what habits to form, we may, by default, end up with the bad ones.

Always be associated with people who are good at heart. You will experience your inner transformation.

Sometimes we don't realize our own strength until someone tries to take advantage of our weakness.

Stop planting flowers in people's yards, when such people aren't going to water them.

***

# Child Parent Relations

A wise man advising his child said, "Make sure you never forget to do these three things:

*Eating the best food.

*Sleeping on the most comfortable bed.

*Residing in the best of homes."

His child replied, "You know we are poor, how can I do that?"

The father replied, "If you eat when you are truly hungry, you will be eating the most delicious food. If you work hard, honestly and sincerely, and go to sleep tired, you will sleep on the most comfortable bed. If you are courteous to people, treat them with dignity and respect, you will reside in their hearts, that is the best residence of all."

It doesn't matter who hurt you, what matters is who made you smile again. While you may have struggled with staying at home, some people wish they had one.

You need to trust your parents in the most crucial stages, a guide you must not mess up with. Try to visualize the consequences of your rash decisions.

Parents must make sure that their children get the best possible food and education as per their capabilities; and be firm, loving, caring and sharing. As they grow, give them more independence and let them do more. Protect them and keep them safe. Inculcate and encourage the family value system and beliefs; they can go a long way.

Until both your parents have passed on, and you have been promoted, so to speak, you remain a child. You must be courteous, thoughtful and respectful towards them. Look after them or else back off if they so desire.

If you are not as fulfilled, happy, prosperous or peaceful as you should be, stop blaming your parents or the economy and take full responsibility for your circumstances especially after your basic education has been provided for. This is the first step to live better.

Resolve to work on changing yourself before you seek to change others. Problems and setbacks are part of life, so try not to hold a fixed view of how things should be; constantly evolve and reflect.

In this world there are no greater, or more adorable deities than one's father and mother.

***

# Fake Relationships

A relationship with a person who only communicates on births and deaths of Individuals is not worth the name, and is selfish to the core. Such persons are best avoided or kept at arm's length.

Review your feelings. Not everyone is happy for you. Time has a wonderful way of showing us what and who really matters to us. Inherent envy may reveal itself and targets of such envy are the ones who are simple, honest and sincere as compared to the ones who steal relationships for greed, or power and quick money. It is also not uncommon to see farce and duplicity, money and muscle power, often hand in hand, attempt subjugation of the simple, honest and sincere. Walk away from people who do not care for you and who are opportunistic. Stop telling people more than they need to know.

Sometimes you may really want to do something but it is unrealistic. Instead of knocking yourself about, cultivate the art of knowing when to walk away and you will find it lot less stressful. Letting go and walking away means you are exercising control and good decision-making powers – you are exercising your options rather than letting the situation overwhelm you. Walk away now and look back after ten years; and I bet you will be hard pushed to even remember what it was all about. A strong person doesn't seek revenge, they just move on.

The selfish individuals in your orbit, may ignore you, until they need you. Some bad experiences prove the value of good ones in life. No matter how good you are, there will be someone who hates you for no reason.

People who do not understand your silence will never understand your words. Just be yourself and carry on.

Don't hesitate to walk away with a smile from things, places and people that leave your soul heavy.

***

# Professional Relationships

There are many advantages of having a positive attitude as it makes for a pleasing personality and leads to productivity in work; while a negative attitude leads to bitterness, resentment and stress.

Stay focused on official work. Avoid too much familiarity at the workplace, it breeds contempt.

Try to let go of small annoyances, and express others calmly. Remember you don't have to react to everything that upsets you.

Your goals must be balanced. In a performance management system, goals are set to align individuals to the organization's strategy and to stretch their performance.

Always have the right Values, Ethics and Benchmarks.

For some the path is rockier than others, but no one reaches anywhere without facing any form of adversity.

The art of life lies in constant re-adjustment to our surroundings. Be flexible – not every situation is covered in the training manual.

Develop impeccable etiquette over time.

***

# Social Relationships

When you grow up in social life, pleasant and unpleasant experiences are going to be part of your life. Life is a journey and you need relationships and people at every turn. Have circles of people and classify them. Humans are social animals on the lookout for satisfying relationships.

Be aware of how you move at a given moment, how you carry yourself in different situations. Your body mirrors your state of mind. Watch your responses. Watch your different states of mind as they arise. Actions often take place without thought; and patterns of behavior are repeated. Self-awareness gives you a different view; you can see the patterns and change them yourself. Keep assessing your emotional well-being.

Relationships vary between different people and different groups. Friends expect us to offer them our support, encouragement and time and the same is also expected from them. There is also a need to develop skills if we are to maintain happy, healthy and rewarding relationships. A relationship can grow stronger depending upon the effort we put in to nurture it. We maintain an emotional bank account, where we can make deposits and withdrawals. If we are able to keep a positive reserve in our relationships, it grows; but if our balance becomes low, bitterness, mistrust and discord will develop.

Improve your social skills. Self-esteem is an individual's subjective evaluation of his own self-worth. It encompasses beliefs about oneself as well as emotional states, such as triumph, despair, pride and shame. Empathy is the ability to sense other people's emotions, coupled with the ability to imagine what someone else might be thinking or feeling. Maintain a positive image. Be proud of your achievements. You should be able to admit mistakes and learn from them. When you rise in life, your friends know who you are. When you fall down, you know who your friends are. Most often social relationships have a life of their own till interests collide or you have major differences.

There is no point in hanging out with people who don't make you feel good.

***

# Marital Relationships

No Man or Woman can ever be perfect; perfection in a person exists only in stories, serials, movies or fairy tales.

Beauty attracts the eye but personality captures the heart. Make your choice. You are lucky if you get both.

Harmony in a relationship, with mutual love, is essential for long term prosperity. We must accept that we all are a bit different and that's what makes us unique. Don't find reasons for all problems. Some problems have to be solved, some to be lived with and some to be ignored.

The only person who listens to both sides of an argument is the fellow in the next apartment – lower the tone.

Understand, respect the differences, aspirations, build up memories, be guides to each other. Fault finding, criticism, magnifying others' small mistakes do not help in a happy union. It is about loyalty and team work.

Try to plan at least one long and two short holidays with the family every year.

In a way, there is nothing called as Love, all things human are fallible. If you have allowed your advisors to run your life, Beware! Never discuss your marital problems with just anyone available.

Marriage marks the beginning of sharing your life with another. Couple relationships grow and develop over time, like a tree; and its development is a long process, a lifelong adventure shared between the partners.

Instead of focusing on the fault look for a remedy. This is the quick one sentence solution. It mostly works.

Saying sorry has many benefits, even if it does stick in your throat a little. It defuses tension, gets rid of bad feelings and clears the air; probably the other partner would apologize too.

No one must engineer or orchestrate a separation between a couple. Two people who are not keen to take the relationship forward, must decently bring it to closure, arrived at mutually with grace.

Marriage vows are often soon forgotten – more so, these days. Marriage as an institution is unfortunately continuing to fail. Unconditional love and support works best.

Assume the harmonious state and hopefully eventually you will find peace and harmony. Putting time and space between you and your troubles does give you a wider view, a better perspective.

If a relationship is coming to its end, instead of playing out long complicated and potentially hurtful games, end it peacefully. Part as friends not enemies.

***

# Financial Relationships

No matter how tall you are, you can never see tomorrow. Identify your needs, savings, wants, debt repayment. Have a reserve fund for emergency like situations.

Save, invest, budget, have varied portfolios, and diversification. Don't be penny wise and pound foolish.

Typically you may have to cater for settling down expenses. Plan to save at least about 30 - 40 % of income for a secure future.

Have a secure Insurance Policy, but not for investment purpose. Know the difference between term plan, endowment plan etc.

The cost of health care is rising and it is impossible to manage it without Medical insurance.

Have your home. Rented places can never give you the security of a home that is yours for keeps. Having a second house which remains vacant mostly, can be costly.

Plan between Debt, Cash, Bonds, Fixed Deposits, Life Insurance, Equity, metals like Gold, Real estate, Shares, Mutual funds and Systematic Investment Plans. Analyze the returns.

Plan your family and solo holidays. There are a number of holiday packages also available. Bond together and click lots of photos and videos as part of your heritage. Life is indeed a series of memories.

You need to either have monthly savings or Education loans for higher studies. The expenses will vary depending upon the choice of profession. The children must also take up part time assignments in case of higher studies and reduce the burden on their parents.

Post retirement, one's focus may shift to giving jobs to others rather than picking up another job. You can do business or consultancy in the field in which you have acquired expertise. Work from home is also an option for the couple.

Periodic expenses can be suitably relooked at and further savings may be possible. Avoid being a victim of lifestyle inflation. Beware of sale discounts. Beware of the effect wherein customers perceive higher priced goods to be worth more, simply because they cost more. You always end up paying more in EMI options.

Have a healthy bank balance. Shortage of money can be demoralizing. Living on credit or borrowing is demeaning and lowers one in one's own eyes. Cater for unforeseen emergencies.

It is said that Takers eat well and Givers sleep well. Only those who will never die or know when they will die, don't need a Will. Have a Will, preferably registered and in the hands of the Executor with sufficient copies as per the rules of the land.

We get water today because someone laid the pipe line. Make your family tree chart from where you can recollect and encourage your descendants to keep adding it on, maybe even a family website.

Now look at it this way. Birth is your opening stock. What comes to you is credit. What goes from you is debit. Death is your closing stock. Your loved ones are your assets. Your bad habits are your liabilities. Your happiness is your profit. Your sorrow is your loss. Your heart is your good will. Your soul is your fixed asset. Your character is your capital. Your knowledge is your investment, age is your depreciation and Karma your Auditor.

***

# Relations – Another Perspective

Not all relationships will endure. Interpersonal relationships are not a business; they are born from a feeling in the heart and not in mind.

Time is precious, make sure you spend it with the right people. Some people who are good from the heart are often rough in speaking out their feelings because they cannot pretend. They just do good when the time comes. This relation cannot be defined in classical terms; it could fall into any of the existing categories, or an entirely new one.

Unexpected wisdom from a bird as the story goes:

*A Man caught a bird. The bird said to him, "Release me, I will give you three valuable pieces of advice. I will give you the first when you let me go, the second when I fly to that branch and the third when I fly up to the top of the tree." The Man agreed and let the bird go. Now free, the bird said, "Do not torture, torment and burden yourself with excessive regrets from past mistakes." The bird then flew up to a branch and said, "Do not believe anything that goes against common sense, unless you have first-hand proof." The bird then flew up to the top of the big tree and said, "You fool, I have two huge jewels inside me. If you would have killed me instead of letting me go, you would have been rich." "Damn it!" the man exclaimed. "How could I be so stupid? I am never going to get over it. Bird can you give me the third piece of advice as consolation?" The bird replied, "I was merely testing you. You are asking for further advice, yet you already disregarded the first two pieces of advice I gave you. Look back; you just tormented yourself with regret for letting me go, and you believed that somehow there are two huge jewels inside a tiny bird like me. So here is your extra advice; if you do not apply what you already know, why are you so intent on gaining what you do not know?"*

*-A Sufi Tale*

Dynamically, there are only two emotions love and fear. All other feelings stem from them.

Conflict comes from unmet needs, and our needs are expressions of fear, demand and attack. When chronic needs and grievances are carried through life, they typically become an obsession.

Sometimes closure arrives years later. Long after you stopped searching for it. You are just sitting there, laughing this laugh that is unapologetically yours; as it trails off, the corners of your mouth hug your face and it hits you. 'I am happy'. It's just like that, with no fanfare or epiphany. Suddenly, you are grateful for the good byes that carried you to this moment; to the space you are holding.

***

# Mind Versus Heart

Mind says move on, it's over. Heart says, hold on, let's try it one more time.

*Good judgment comes from experience, and experience, well that comes mostly from poor judgment.*

*- Rita Mae Brown*

No response is a response and it is a powerful one.

Don't cry for someone who killed your smile. The world is going to judge you anyways, so live your life the way you feel right.

Take your thoughts into a quiet place, let your intuition and intellect – rather than your emotions look at the situation. Never reply when you are angry. Never make a promise when you are happy. And never make a decision when you are sad.

When you fully trust someone without any doubt, you finally get either a Person for Life or a Lesson for Life.

***

# *Chapter 7:*
# *Routine Daily Chores*

Today holds infinite possibilities. This is yet another day to make or waste. This day is a beautiful gift to find the treasure of happiness, achieve small milestones of life. Life is an unwrapped gift; open it gently, unfold it. Life is not perfect or tailor made; you may have many unseen challenges today. Try and keep your movements aligned with the Sun.

Every day is a new beginning. Every day starts with some expectations and ends with some experience. Each moment in a day has its own value. Morning brings hope. Afternoon brings faith. Evening brings Love. Night brings Rest. Leave a little space for yourself while you do absolutely nothing to recharge and repair yourself.

You are blessed to take another day to feel the Sun's rays as nature's greatest miracle. Be mindful of the things you put into your body physically, emotionally and spiritually.

***

## Morning Wake Up

Wake up each day and be thankful for life. Someone somewhere else may be fighting to survive.

Every morning is a symbol of rebirth of our life, so forget all yesterday's bad moments and make today the most beautiful day of your life.

Some get sleep cycle peaks at about 3 am or 4 am and the body gradually wakes up. Lots of people set alarms with the best of intentions but hit the snooze and eventually run late. The key lies inside our body, which is the body clock. According to 'National Institute of General Medical Sciences' (NIGMS), the body's master clock is located in the brain, which produces and regulates our circadian rhythms, which in turn, help determine sleep patterns over the course of a twenty-four-hour period. Irregular rhythms have been linked to chronic health conditions such as Obesity, Diabetes, Depression, Bipolar Disorder and Seasonal Affective Disorder. There are ways to re-calibrate your system to get the sleep you need and wake up feeling refreshed and ready for the day ahead. Sound sleep is very essential.

Morning brings hope. Wake up drill must consist of getting up early with a bang! Stretch, Smile, Thank your Creator, be raring to go with enthusiasm.

Start your day with a deep breath. Inhale all the love and goodness, and exhale all the tears, fears, worries, and stress. Wake up with smile on your face.

Look into the mirror and say you are great. Splash your face with water, swish and rinse your mouth. Drink a glass of room temperature water. Clear your bowels. Brush your teeth, clean your tongue, massage your gums. Rub your head gently.

Morning is the best time to remember all your idols in the world who make you happy. Open the curtains and windows.

Play your favorite songs. Sacred chants for a while help you to think and reflect consciously.

Do what pleases you – be it exercise, meditation, yoga. Prepare a 'Must Do' list for the day. Don't get disappointed if you can't follow your routine on a particular day; but don't give up, and bounce back stronger. Consider yourself a machine with a built-in timer so you can wake up to the smell of freshly brewed coffee or whatever your choice be.

Do not start your day with looking up messages in your mobile, make it wait – else it gets compulsive and consumes much time and precious energy. Rather read a book, listen to positive talk, make it a ritual to consume words of wisdom for at least fifteen minutes every day.

Develop the habit of getting up early and sitting in silence. After reading a peaceful thought reflect on it. Leave yourself notes.

Transformation begins when empowering ideas enter your mind every day, consistently. Most importantly do what the clock does, keep moving.

***

# Freshening Up

Sort your clothes and finish all your preparations the night before. Maximize your morning bathroom efficiency. Keep your accessories by the door. Use the bathroom first. Commence your grooming routine. Have a place for everything. The Washroom is a place which should be clean, aesthetically decorated to one's liking with good lighting effect, which can create an overall atmosphere of immaculate cleanliness, orderliness and a place where you don't desist going. Go through your activities deliberately with some margin for extra time. Do not think of your day's activities or watch your mobile. Just maintain a silent atmosphere or play some soothing instrumental music. Let your body feel totally relaxed and at ease.

***

# Morning Exercising

Exercising in the morning has been linked to greater productivity and lowering of blood pressure. It also speeds up a person's metabolism which can improve calorie burning throughout the day. Exercise done on an empty stomach leads to more fat burn than done after meal. One can also practice deep breathing exercises or yoga. Some form of exercise is very essential to get started the right way; the balance, if any, can be done later in the day.

Take a thirty minute to one hour walk every day in fresh air and while you walk, smile. It is the ultimate antidepressant. Remember, in a sound body rests a sound mind. Stretches are very useful and so are essential bodyweight exercises. Look forward to your morning physical activities with vigour.

***

# Meals

Wash your hands well with soap and rinse them dry with a clean towel before approaching your food.

Thank God for your meal which many won't be privileged to have – even as you eat, feel blessed.

The food we eat should provide the nourishment to our body needs. We sometimes put our body systems under too much strain by eating the wrong foods and in excess of actual needs.

To nourish your body avoid using food to satisfy your greed. Chew well and do not swallow. Experts say, that you need to chew each mouthful at least ten times or more depending upon the nature of its content.

Ideally, stomach space must be filled with food up to its half capacity; one fourth to be left for water and the balance for air.

Oral care is the practice of keeping one's mouth clean and free of disease and bad breadth. Treat it with the seriousness it deserves and try to brush after every meal. The culture of carrying a pocket brush to office hardly exists.

Have a balanced diet. Essential nutrients required by the body are Carbohydrates, Proteins, Fats, Vitamins and Minerals. Make your diet chart and follow it.

Consume lesser quantities of carbonated drinks, refined sugar, artificial sweeteners, processed foods.

Don't use mobiles and other gadgets while eating. Keep the ritual sacred and focused.

As you grow in age, eat lighter foodstuffs, especially at night.

Develop the quality to ultimately transform the food you consume into sweet thoughts, words and deeds.

***

# Water Management

Avoid too much water along with food. Have more water after a gap of about half an hour. Drink at least ten glasses of water daily. Drinking water at a certain time maximizes its effect on the body. Two glasses of water after waking up, helps activate internal organs. One glass of water thirty minutes before a meal, helps digestion. One glass of water before bathing, helps to lower blood pressure. One glass of water before bed, also helps prevent leg cramps at night. The leg muscles look for moisture when they contract and wake you up with a Charlie horse (calf cramp). You feel less thirsty with age, beware of it and keep the sipping schedule going. You can put a suitable reminder on your phone if you desire.

There are many Hydration apps providing daily water tracker reminders. Setting alarms is a noisier option, but it works.

***

# Breakfast

Breakfast is the first meal taken after rising from a night's sleep in the morning before undertaking the day's work. Breakfast decreases appetite, reduces hunger and cravings throughout the day. The best time is between 7 am to 9 am. Your digestive system is the strongest in the morning. Eat a hearty meal but never over eat. Listen to your system, it never lies.

There are super delicacies to choose from, some of which are Continental, English, American and South Indian. Choose different options every day.

You may find it useful to add sprouted dal, fresh fruits, oats, nuts and other healthy foods. Quantity of Tea / Coffee if consumed must be minimum.

***

## Take Off

Do not sleep walk through the day. Open your eyes to everything and be fully engaged in all your activities.

Practice a 'no-thought' zone. When you observe silence, you actually recharge your spirit and make way for abundance to enter and keep you centered on higher priorities. Maintain your vertebral column straight. When you keep the backbone straight, energy flows upward and you maintain your awareness. Carry your meditative mind with you, be receptive to your highest good. Remember the famous Japanese proverb: *Hurry but slowly*.

Cherish a thoughtful gesture. Indulge a bit in it. Smile.

***

# Driving

When you step out of the house, risk is inevitable. Start early, stay safe.

Keep full attention if driving. Keep your mobile on silent mode. Attend to only important calls though blue tooth speakers. Do not panic.

Slow down. Speed gives you less time to react and increases the severity of a possible road accident.

Carry a copy of your documents including insurance, pollution control and others, in hard and soft copy formats. Seat belts for four wheelers is for your additional safety. Play some soothing meditation music or tones of positivity. Follow the traffic rules. Do not blow the horn unnecessarily.

If you come across some forms of accident don't start fighting – commonly referred to as 'Road Rage'. There is no need to be naïve. Bad things happen, and often such happenings are beyond your control. Be thankful if you are alive. Always keep in mind, negativity is destructive, regardless of where it originates from. Make every effort to turn it around. Help the injured and needy; even the Law protects you now, so don't hesitate. Keep your personal safety kit.

The road you use safely on a daily basis, is the same road where many others might have lost their precious lives. Be grateful.

***

# At The Office

Enter with a smile. Worship your work station as you may feel comfortable in your mental thoughts. Doing the most ordinary task mindfully lets you notice each moment as it unfolds.

Take stock, plan, delegate and achieve targets. It encompasses all sub activities.

Stay ahead of requirements. It is a great virtue to possess.

Make a motivated team, focus on training, be result oriented, be compassionate, be friendly but firm.

If you stay positive in a negative situation you win. The right attitude never takes you in a wrong direction.

Take plenty of fluids, less of tea or coffee. Avoid heavy snacks. Short periods of inner quiet will refresh your mind and body even if it is work from home.

See your troubles as blessings and transform them into stepping stones. Take them as opportunities.

***

# Lunch

The abbreviation for luncheon, is the meal eaten around mid-day, commonly the second meal of the day, after breakfast. The meal varies in size depending on culture and significant variations exist in different areas of the world. It needs to be light and balanced. There should be a gap of five to six hours to allow the last meal to be digested. Chewing properly is very essential. It has to be performed as a ritual. Heavy lunch can interfere with your concentration and work efficiency. It is also best to eat when hungry.

Packed lunch gets cold, keep food warming arrangements in place. Alternatively, freshly prepared warm food can also be consumed.

Cut out your thinking chord while you relish your meal whether Roti, Rice, Dal, Vegetables, Pizza, Sandwiches, Meat or Salads.

***

# Tea And Snacks

It is important to snack on things that are filled with real food and nourishing ingredients that will leave you feeling energized and happy.

Healthy snacks could be pumpkin seeds, sprouts, peanuts or a couple of healthy biscuits.

Tea could be Green, Black, Herbal, or Masala tea. Generally, more than two to three cups a day would not be advisable.

Coffee is a brewed drink prepared from roasted coffee beans. Dried coffee seeds are roasted to varying degrees, depending on the desired flavor.

Use natural forms of sugar as much as possible, rather than refined polished sugar. You can try Jaggery powder, honey or other natural sugars.

***

# Back Home

Depending on context, here it refers to being back at your place of residence, essentially, to your own little private space or nest.

Have an Energy drink like hot cocoa. Spend a few minutes in solitude. Share a few notes with your partner in your balcony, garden or living room space of your house.

Consider Gardening, Exercise, Yoga, Zumba, Games and Sports. It leads to significant amount of increase in energy levels and stamina, increases resistance to stress and also aids in good sleep.

However, working out too close to bedtime could make it harder to fall asleep as body temperature, metabolism and heart rate are elevated, by aerobic activity and strength training. Those who think they have no time for bodily exercise will sooner or later have to find time for illness.

Freshen up again in a slightly more relaxed manner.

Your faculties need stimulation of sorts. It is a good time to pray and do some meditation. Doing meditation may also be followed by Reiki. Follow it with your own leisure time activities like playing musical instruments, reading light stuff, arts and craft, writing, or anything that makes you forget your worries and time and makes you smile, laugh and relaxed.

Make use of Laughter therapy. Watch comic shows. Laugh and make others laugh. Spread happiness.

***

# Dinner

Dinner is a meal which the family must have together on a common table. After breakfast the family separates and generally unites during dinner time. Favorite dishes of members can be prepared in rotation.

The best memories are made around the table. Families that eat together stay together.

Eat light; soups and salads are desirable add ons.

Have a great ambience and soft music while you eat and gently converse.

The dinner table is the center for the teaching and practicing not just table manners but conversation, consideration, tolerance, family feeling.

***

# After Dinner

Go for an after-dinner walk, or within your colony or terrace. Play indoor games like a round of cards, carom or have a reading session. Clean yourself up and clean up your junk email, because it is said that the blue light after dinner also affects quality of sleep.

Review your responses to situations. To purify your responses with improved awareness, make it sink into your sub conscious.

A good laugh followed by a long sleep is the best cure for anything.

***

# Thanks-Giving Prayer

All family members should pray preferably together and call it a day with a sense of deep gratitude. Appreciate the little blessings you received through the day. It also gives you a chance to focus on what matters most and letting go anything that caused you to get upset. It also bonds the family together.

***

# Sleep

Most of us sleep far more than we require to, it may need real introspection. Set dim lights, perfume, fresh air circulation, clean bed sheets. Before going to bed, sit quietly and recollect the events of the day, running through them in your mind like a film reflecting on what actions of ours went in the wrong direction and what were right. Remind yourself of your important work of the next day and set your human alarm clock. Make up, smile and go to bed. Play the music of your choice to induce yourself to sleep.

Sleep in total darkness. When there is little or no light at night your clock tells the brain to make more melatonin, a hormone which makes you sleepy.

You are going into another world; you can live there the way you wish and make up for what you don't have in real life. Strengthen your imaginative skills.

Sleep in a direction other than head facing north. Turn to sideways or lie straight like a kingly sleep, few are fortunate to be able to do that. The best hours of sleep are from 9 pm to 4 am. The Magnetic force of Sun enters the earth from the east side and if we sleep so, it enters our head from the East and exits through the feet, leading to cool heads and warm feet. Develop a regular bed time if possible.

Don't sleep directly under the fan. It is best to have natural air circulation through meshing.

Try coconut oil massage on the soles of your feet before sleeping at night. This makes one sleep better and relieves fatigue.

# Weekly Rest Day Routine

Awaken a little later than usual. Take a relaxing walk preferably outside, like a solitary one on the beach or the hill side. It is good for the heart and also reduces anxiety and improves mood. Don't carry your worries with you.

Experience and feel the sight, sounds and smells.

Have a leisurely bath and a good breakfast of a favorite item. Try to get morning sunlight for at least half an hour. It nourishes and energizes the human body, increases resistance to infections, increases metabolism, provides vital minerals and much more.

Catch up on reading; plan a movie at home or outside. Call a distant friend or two. Connect with past pleasant memories, replenish your goals, strengthen your capabilities. Nurture some plants, smile at a stranger, bird feed, visit and help an orphanage. If you happen to go out in solitude, try shouting out and release your pent-up feelings, you will feel liberated.

Indulge in foot soaking in hot / lukewarm / cold water with rock salt. It relieves the pent-up stress.

Use time to introspect and get your answers silently. Keep off worries. I would even advocate one day in a month to be on silent mode to invigorate our energy system.

Maintain your weekly digest. Feel in control.

Take it slow and give your soul a chance to catch up with your body.

*****

# Chapter 8:

# Physical Health Management

*Only staying active will make you want to live hundred years -*
*Japanese Proverb.*

Our life is a whole, consisting of body, mind and pure consciousness. Both health and disease have psychological as well as physical origins.

Illness may begin in the mind with emotions and then effect the physical body; similarly, physical disorders can generate mental ones.

A regular daily routine, nourishing diet, positive emotions and loving relationships result in strength and health.

Food is fuel that drives our bodies. The maintenance of pH level of blood within a healthy range is imperative.

Ensure that your basic parameters including Vitamin D, B-12 remain at the requisite levels and include annual blood tests to keep your metabolic health in check. Check for history of good health patterns like sleep, indigestion, acidity and cravings. One needs to specially guard against Obesity, Hypertension, Diabetes and Depression with growing age. Have a family Doctor who is well versed with your ailment and its history. Have your medicines in a timely manner; order online from authentic suppliers. Be in touch with the specialists that you may need to consult.

The key to remaining healthy is awareness. If you know the condition of your constitution you can gauge how your mind, body and emotions respond to the changing conditions in your environment. Potential causes of illness and imbalance are constantly rising, both within us and outside us.

There is a connection between the heart and brain. Omega-3 Fatty Acids work on optimizing cardiovascular health by reduction of plaque in the arteries, reduction of mental fatigue and promoting brain cell performance.

Ayurveda and Naturopathy provide us with the knowledge to prevent a disease and to eliminate its root cause; but they are largely preventive, while other therapies are curative.

It is better and easier to move from body fitness to mind fitness and beyond.

***

# Physical Exercises

Strength is life, weakness is death. Always aspire to stay fit. A workout is a personal triumph over laziness and procrastination.

*Lack of activity destroys the good condition of every human being, while movement and methodical physical exercise save it and preserve it.*

*- Plato*

Exercise daily, to maximum capacity in cooler weather and reduce the intensity and duration during on days when it is too hot. Even strong people get tired, don't overdo anything.

You should ensure that you remain well-hydrated while working out — especially in hot and dry climates where sweating takes the form of invisible sweating.

Treadmill and cycling be a good combination with light warming up and cooling down exercises. Your body is a reflection of your lifestyle. Strength training is more important for slowing the ageing of the physical body. This does not mean you use heavy weights; resistance bands, using own body weight are also tremendously helpful and cannot be excluded. You need to vary workouts as per your bodily needs. Core strength is critical as you age; it builds bone density and enhances balance both of which prevent accidents like fractures.

On days you miss your workout, watch a video or dance class, don't let your routine and momentum get weak or discarded. Fitness is like a relationship; you can't cheat on it and expect it to work.

Do something today that your self will thank you for.

***

# Sports

Sports provide a fine form of exercise with multiple health benefits. Everyone must aspire to develop skills in at least two games and reach some reasonable level of proficiency. Take time out; if not every day, maybe thrice a week. Our entire entity just loves sports, go and explore. There is so much to choose from right from those that demand higher physical endurance to lighter ones.

Sports teaches you to understand the meaning of team work. You can experience the fun of competition towards a common goal and at the same time build your character. You get to learn self-discipline, healthy competition, being gracious in victory and defeat, importance of being a part of team and understanding your role.

Real sporting activities are also great relievers of mental fatigue, besides physical benefits, whether Football, Basketball, Athletics, Cycling, Swimming and many others. You learn to be a Winner in life.

Sports are the epitome of hard work and dedication. It is also about those incredible moments when sheer human will and desire overcomes the odds.

*** 

# Regular Monitoring of Health

Health is a precious asset that we don't recognize, acknowledge and appreciate until it has been depleted.

There is no defeat except in no longer trying. A Psychosomatic disorder is a disease or affliction which involves both mind and body. In the true sense all diseases can be connected with state of mind. Some directly related to factors such as stress, among others are hypertension, diabetes, heart disease, stomach ulcers, eczema, psoriasis, and obesity. These conditions may be can be triggered off or worsened by the status of your mental health. Even some types of Cancer are caused by thought patterns of the mind.

Feelings of fear, guilt, criticism and resentment cause more problems than any other environmental factors. Mind body healing is a new form of therapy. You can change the negative thought patterns of past and present day by various techniques including Neuro Linguistic Programming. The heart works without any rest for years; keep it always healthy and happy.

Modern consumerist lifestyle trends, are largely responsible for diabetes and heart disease striking at an age, as young as thirty-five years. Even forms of cancer like colonic cancer and breast cancer are increasingly identified as being linked to intake of red meat, alcohol and tobacco; and are included as life style diseases. Lack of exercise, increased disposable income, easily available loans give access to the 'good life'.

Therefore, at a reasonable time from early middle-age onwards, do check your Blood Sugar and Blood pressure often. Reduce intake of salt, sugar, dairy and starchy products.

***

# Health and Safety – Senior Citizens

Caring for seniors is perhaps the greatest responsibility we have towards those who made possible the life that we enjoy today.

Seniors need to avoid climbing stairs, turning around too fast, bending over your feet, wearing pants while standing, sit ups, turning the waist left and right, stepping backward, bending to lift heavy items, suddenly standing up, straining / tweezing too hard.

Don't sit on bed and watch TV for long periods. Don't wait till you are hungry to eat. Don't wait till you are thirsty to drink. Don't wait till you are sleepy to sleep. Don't wait till you feel tired to rest. Don't wait till you fall sick to go for a medical checkup otherwise you only will regret it; no one else.

The cause of Mental confusion could be a result of uncontrolled diabetes when the person becomes hypoglycemic, urinary infection or dehydration. Make use of adult diapers if required.

The elderly stop feeling thirsty and consequently stop drinking fluids, which is a part of the natural ageing process. Keep yourself well hydrated especially during the day.

Companionship is vital for survival.

***

# Allergies

Allergy is a damaging immune response by the body to a substance, especially to a particular food, pollen, fur, dust to which it has become hyper sensitive.

Allergies begins with a means of expelling toxins and parasites faster than the traditional immune system. Some allergies appear at young age and go away after a few years, while others come at a later stage and may even stay for a life time. For instance an allergic bronchitis can vanish after a couple of seasons; and likewise one may later develop gluten or lactose intolerance.

Keep a track of your health, bowels, state of mind and monitor them. It is not difficult if you keep your awareness level high. Sometimes anxiety and fear of an allergic reaction can induce allergy like physical symptoms. There are inhaled, ingested, contact allergies.

You need to distinguish between an allergy and intolerance. While some children outgrow allergies usually those to eggs and wheat, many retain them or even develop later in life.

*** 

# Medication

Couples can take care of each other. For single people you may need a special attendant or support from safe ecosystems created for senior citizens.

Have your medicines on time. Keep some system to remind yourself. Opening your medicines and placing them in front of you before you start your meals is a good method to avoid forgetting or taking a double dose.

 Order your stock well in advance, through apps or reliable stores.  Don't miss your regular medicines. Keep a First Aid box and general medicine stock for emergencies. Prefer Strips with days of week mentioned for easy reference.

Avoid medicines with cold water. Don't lie down immediately after taking medicines.

Display your Ambulance number and be in touch with your family Doctor.

Nowadays, one can directly go to specialists or super specialists of their choice provided they have sufficient knowledge of their problem and basics of medical science. Keep yourself updated about your problems and dosage of medicines prescribed.

Self-diagnosis must be avoided and likewise information on Google must be at best used for gaining knowledge or clarification on medical issues, or medicines, but not for starting you own treatment as such.

***

# Diet

It is essential to have breakfast early, lunch on time and dinner early. Chew well, taking about thirty minutes to eat a meal.

Nutrition is a very important part of health. Eat a balanced diet full of fruits, salads, vegetables, carbohydrates, proteins, fats, vitamins, minerals.

Do not indulge in heavy binge eating, especially, non-vegetarian food. Eating a small meal every 3-4 hours will help maintaining your basic metabolic rate at its appropriate biological level.

Use healthy spices with benefits; such as Cinnamon, Clove, Cumin, Black Cardamom, Saffron, Black pepper, Nutmeg, Turmeric and others.

Unsaturated fats should be taken in preference to saturated fats.

Refined foods like sugar should be cut down. Salt intake should be minimal.

Food should be fresh, well cooked and served hot.

# Water

Pure water is the world's first and foremost medicine. Drinking water at the correct time maximizes its effectiveness on the human body.

Drinking about two glasses of water after waking up helps activate the internal organs. One glass of water 30 minutes before meals helps digestion. One glass of water before bathing helps lower blood pressure. One glass of water before bed can prevent stroke and leg cramps at night.

 Water can also be drunk from a copper vessel for better benefits. Water can also be charged with sunlight. Water can be stored in coloured glass bottles for different ailments according to corresponding chakras such as blue for throat problems, green for love, healing, yellow for digestive ailments etc.

Bless the drinking water with positive affirmations before you consume, whenever possible.

Drink more water. Your skin, your hair, your mind and your body will thank you. Drink more water during the day and lesser at night.

***

# Fasting

Fasting is truly a secret source of power. Health and healing follow fasting.

In spite of so much to eat, fasting is considered healthy. Have you tried it as a time-tested method?

Fast occasionally such as, skipping a full meal or having a salt free day, oil free day, sugar free day, only warm water day.

Fasting is a powerful therapeutic process that can help people recover from mild to severe health conditions. It also gives the digestive tract time to completely rest and strengthen its mucosal lining.

It has been linked to a wide array of potential health benefits, including weight loss, as well as improved blood sugar control, heart health, brain function and cancer prevention.

 Take medical advice before fasting if you have complicated health issues.

Fasting also cleans the soul, raises the mind, subjects one's flesh to the spirit, renders the heart contrite and humble, scatters the clouds of concupiscence, quenches the fire of lust and kindles the true light of chastity.

Fasting is futile unless it is accompanied by an incessant longing for self-restraint.

Happy fasting!

***

# Chapter 9:
# Mental Health Management

The structure of the brain is known to undergo changes, as it loses roughly a million neurons a year with age. Physical illness is also a direct cause of psychiatric symptoms. When people become physically ill, they may feel anxious, depressed or angry; usually this emotional reaction is of a transient nature.

Some common symptoms which may be due to physical illness are depression, anxiety, fatigue, weakness, low moods, disturbed behavior, headache and loss of weight. Burdens can weigh you down if they manage to engulf you.

It is hard to free someone who is caged in their own self. Cages aren't made of iron; they're made of your own thoughts. Free yourself ASAP.

When something doesn't go our way, we get agitated and sad. Whatever is happening outside is not in our control, but we can control our response to it. Even if something continues to bother you, divert your mind by any creative activity. Endeavor to move on.

The body benefits from movement, and the mind benefits from stillness.

Don't compare your life with others, everyone's starting point and end point are so different.

Don't let anyone's ignorance, hate, drama, or negativity stop you from being the best person you can be.

A very important and challenging part of our lives is managing our thoughts and feelings in keeping with how we want them to be.

We infer motives from our observation of behavior. Maslow claims motives are of hierarchical importance as below. As our lower motives are relatively satisfied, we become aware of our higher motives.

 The commonly accepted Hierarchy of Needs higher to lower are:

✓ Self Actualization.

✓ Self Esteem.

✓ Love and Belongingness.

✓ Safety and Security.

Read Autobiographies of Great Men in professions that you admire. You will certainly find lessons from the lives and experiences of characters, good or bad.

 Avoid toxic people. Everyone doesn't need access to your inner kingdom. Some people may be draining you and you don't even realize it. You are allowed to say 'No'. You are allowed to not answer calls. You are allowed to break plans, and save your interests.

The COVID pandemic has brought about a long lockdown across the world in recent times, indeed unparalleled. Instead of treating this as a period of isolation and quarantine, let us look at it as one of rejuvenation and inner growth.

Knowledge speaks while wisdom listens. The strongest factor for success is self-esteem. Believe you can do it; believe you deserve it and believe you can get it.

Mental Health Management is no more a taboo and more and more people are being open about it, seeking professional help, guidance and moving on with their lives.

***

## Stress

Stress is the physical, mental, emotional reaction to any change that requires an adjustment or response. It can come from any event or thought that makes you feel frustrated, angry or nervous; causing higher levels of anxiety.

Emotions are responses of arousal that have a survival value in evolution that can be suppressed or repressed, and communicated through verbal as well as non-verbal means.

The response to stimuli differs from person to person. Pressure may be from inner or outer sources depending on pressure, frustration or conflict.

Anxiety is a vague subjective awareness of a threat not clearly perceived. Fear is more specific and objective danger.

Anger is a strong feeling of annoyance, displeasure or hostility. Rage is uncontrollable anger.

Guilt is when we have violated our conscience, our internal standards of good and bad.

Chronic stress can often lead to Depression and many more illnesses, both physical and mental. There is a need to increase tolerance levels in most people.

What is Stress? It is the gap between our expectation and reality. The greater the gap, the greater the stress; so, expect nothing and accept everything.

Do regular stretches, it relieves tension. Sing a song along with your radio. Keep your routine, do not overthink, meditate. Be passionately involved in a single activity for a couple of hours; call someone. Build up your finances and see them grow. Spread happiness.

***

# Depression

Depression is a condition where a person has feelings of severe despondency and dejection. Clinical Depression is characterized by persistently depressed mood or loss of interest in activities, causing significant impairment in daily lives.

Stress, anxiety, sadness, worries all lead to Depression.

Conditions that get worse due to depression include Arthritis, Asthma, Cardiovascular disease, Cancer, Diabetes, Obesity. Symptoms may be ongoing or may come and go like moods; emptiness, sadness, loss of interest, concentration problems, fatigue, digestive problems, sleeplessness. These may be triggered by stressful events such as loss of a loved one, divorce, separation, economic problems etc.

Living with depression can be difficult, but treatment can help improve your quality of life. Talk to your healthcare provider about possible options. It is common to combine medical treatments and lifestyle therapies. Speaking with a therapist can help you learn skills to cope with negative feelings.

Have adequate supplements of vitamin B and vitamin D. Omega 3 works on optimizing your cardiovascular health by reduction of plaque in the arteries and reduction of mental fatigue and promoting brain cell performance. Exercise regularly, smile, laugh, sleep well, build strong relationships and discard the evil ones.

Stop being always available to people who are just there for you when it's convenient for them.

Depression and anxiety may occur in a person at the same time; and may produce several similar symptoms that may be short term or long term. Be considerate towards others who are suffering, you never know when it might be your turn to face a similar situation.

***

# Memory Deterioration, Senility, Dementia

The general causes of the above, other than aging, include medications, alcohol, tobacco, drug use, sleep deprivation, depression, stress, nutritional deficiency, head injury and stroke.

 Senility is the physical and mental decline associated with old age, especially physical strength, memory and alertness loss.

Dementia is a syndrome in which there is deterioration of memory, thinking, behavior and ability to perform everyday activities. Common symptoms include losing track of time and place, increased need of assistance, difficulty in recognizing familiar people and places, behavioral changes, communication blockages etc.

***

# Bipolar Disorder

It is a disorder associated with episodes of mood swings ranging from depressive lows to highs characterized by episodes of Mania. The exact cause is not known, but a combination of genetics (history), environment and altered brain structure and chemistry may play a role. Serotonin imbalance is one of the bio-chemical causes of Depression. Such mental illness may be an important factor in job loss and family discord. With any type of bipolar disorder, misuse of drugs and alcohol use can lead to more episodes and may require help from a specialist who can address both issues. Teenagers and others use the word 'bipolar' to describe their love life, or the absurd. A parent or anyone in family with a true bipolar disorder is a stressful matter, it often crosses borders with conditions like mania, schizophrenia and other psychoses.

***

# Schizophrenia

Schizophrenia is characterized by thoughts or experiences that seem out of touch with reality, diagnosed speech or behavior and difficulty in concentration and memory. The causes are similar to those of bipolar disorder. Symptoms may include delusions, hallucinations, bizarre behavior, paucity of speech and disorganized thinking. Treatment is usually life long and involves a combination of medications, psychotherapy and coordinated care.

# Alzheimer's Disease

Alzheimer's Disease is a progressive disease that destroys memory and other important mental functions as the brain cells themselves degenerate and die. It is also called senile dementia.

Although your loved one may not remember you or might do things that frustrate you, this is the time when he or she needs you the most.

There is no effective treatment for this disease. The tongue exercise is believed to help control and prevent Alzheimer's Disease. Stretch out your tongue and move it to the right then to the left for ten times. It is believed to stimulate the brain and keep you healthy. Of critical importance in its prevention is keeping mental faculties active by reading stimulating material, doing quizzes, crosswords, sudoku or other puzzles.

*** 

# Counseling

Counseling is a collaborative effort between the Counselor and the Client. Professional Counselors help clients identify goals and potential solutions to problems which cause emotional turmoil; seek to improve communication and coping skills, strengthen self-esteem and promote behavioral change and optimal mental health.

The goals of Counseling may be described as immediate, long range and process goals. Counseling may be Individual Counseling or Group Counseling. They types of Counseling may range from Individual, Student, Career, Matrimonial, Parental, Vocational adjustment and many more.

Psychotherapy and Counseling often complement each other and are used for milder forms of mental disorder or follow through, or supportive treatment after long-term treatment under a psychiatrist. It uses both conscious and unconscious processes and tries to integrate both into a smooth functioning so that the individual acts in an integrated manner. It is a unique treatment activity in that it is performed by individuals with varying professional backgrounds and training.

Health does not come from nutritious food, vitamins and medicines alone. It comes from peace of mind, peace in the heart and soul. For humans with a higher vibration, infection is a minor irritant that is soon eliminated. The reasons for low vibration could be fear, phobia, suspicion, anxiety, stress, tension, jealousy, anger, rage, hate, greed, attachment or pain.

Every thought that comes to your mind must be controlled. It has been aptly said that Mind is a terrible master but a wonderful servant. Hence to focus the mind you need to exercise mind control. Mind can create hell out of heaven and heaven out of hell. If the mind is uncontrolled, it may weaken your determination, cause stress, create depression, hypertension, and may have many other cataclysmic influences.

Watch your thoughts. Be disciplined. Say 'No' to temptations. Live in the present. Be happy.

Mind and intelligence are separate. The mind is not clearly as strong as the intelligence and it only needs to be controlled. An idle mind is a devil's workshop. Chase out unwanted and excess thoughts out of your mind. Also avoid entry into the past, only go to reach out to happy moments. Gratitude revives your brain to be happier.

There is an abundance of energy in negativity. Find a way to re channel that energy in a more positive direction.

Have positive auto suggestions like I can do it and not like I am too tired or it can wait. Our mind can be trained the way we want. Joys, suffering, tensions all originate in the mind. In fact, we live in the mind and with the mind all the time. A happy life is just a sting of happy moments. Joy is never tomorrow; it is always now.

*Viktor Frankl, one of the great psychiatrists of the twentieth century in his book "Mans's Search for Meaning" narrated a story. There was this woman who called him in the middle of the night to calmly inform him she was about to commit suicide. Frankl kept her on the phone and talked her through her depression, giving her reason after reason to carry on living. Finally, she promised she would not take her life, and she kept her word. Later he asked her which reason had persuaded her to live? None of them, she told him. Then what influenced her to go on living he pressed? Her answer was simple, it was Frankl's willingness to listen to her in the middle of the night. A world in which there was someone ready to listen to another's* pain *seemed to her a world in which it was worthwhile to live.* Suicide is not a solution but a greater misery. Go through the pain and outlive it, complete your normal course of journey, don't cut it short. Out of your vulnerabilities will come your strength.

Often, it is not the brilliant argument that makes a difference. Sometimes it is the small act of listening is the greatest gift we can give. Let's hear the cry and reach out to the one in need.

The Corona Virus pandemic related lock down has forced us to have time to think about many privileges, and thank Almighty for the blessings of a breath of fresh air and practice activity in its various colors. We suffer from quarantine and curfew which is hopefully for a limited time, while have we given a thought to the fact there are millions who have lived their entire lives in quarantine state due to their handicap, illness, loneliness etc.

There is a philosophy called the Kupler Rose Model which says that when you go through any tragedy, natural disaster, accident you pass through five stages, these are:

-Denial: Refusal to believe such a thing ever happened or will happen to us.

- Anger: Strong feeling of annoyance, hostility.

- Bargain: Inwardly lamenting that less damage should have occurred.

- Depression: Feeling low due to unexpected turn of events. It can impair all aspects including personal relationships, performance at work and enjoyment of leisure activities.

- Acceptance: It is the last stage. The other way round is to accept it.

A wise person will go straight from the first level to the fifth level and take steps to progress in life. He who is trapped without reaching the fifth stage may need help. Seek the professional help of Psychologists, therapists if need be, but remember understanding is an art and not everyone is an artist.

Not everyone who needs mental help is mentally ill or clinically suffering from psychosis. Some only need support to get back on track. No one should be frowned upon; they are suffering an illness. Be sympathetic and compassionate towards the less privileged.

Mental clarity, insight and mindful actions illuminate all areas of your daily life and relationships.

There are specialized areas of counseling such as Couple's Counseling, Career and Professional Growth Counseling, Performance Counseling, Rehabilitation Counseling, Mental Health Counseling, Substance Abuse Counseling and more; reach out for it.

Develop a sense of humor. Happiness hormones boost immunity. Respect your body when it is asking you for a break. Respect your mind when it is seeking rest. Honor yourself when you need a moment for yourself.

Self-esteem is at the core of healing because of the body mind connect, cellular immunity. If you love yourself, you will develop confidence and healing power.

Self-care is choosing not to argue with people who are committed to misunderstanding you. To protect your internal energy,

# It is okay to cancel a commitment.

# It is okay not to answer a call.

\# It is okay to change your mind.

\# It is okay if you want to be alone.

\# It is okay to take a day off.

\# It is okay to do nothing sometimes.

\# It is okay to speak up.

And lastly, it is okay to let go…

***

# *Chapter 10:*

# *A Few Alternate Therapies For Holistic Health*

## Naturopathy

This art of healing with the help of nature is the gift of our ancient civilization. Probably our forbearers were inspired by the birds and animals which stay closer to nature. For instance, if an animal is sick, it avoids food till it feels better. Dogs and cats eat grass when they want to vomit out the toxins. A Naturopath may use pulse diagnosis and blood reports to begin with.

The application and practice of Naturopathy is not symptomatic in its approach; therefore, any healthy person can also follow it. It has been found useful in the treatment of diabetes, hormonal disorders and hypertension because it cures the root cause of disorders.

Healing agents are found in abundance in natural forces: Air, Water, Mud, Sunlight, Fasting and Rest. Plenty of home remedies from common food ingredients can be prepared and consumed for good health and recovery.

Consumption of bad quality food coupled with lack of exercise causes clogging of blood vessels. The respiratory organs get congested, skin becomes dry or oily, the liver gets congested and fatty or even cirrhotic from over consumption of unhealthy food as well as alcohol, bowels become constipated and toxins from the excreta get reabsorbed in the circulation. Refined white sugar and its various forms is bad for physical as well as mental health and are quite addictive too.

Naturopaths also suggest avoiding food items such as inflammatory oils, canned foods, microwavable foods, corn syrup, refined products such as white rice, maida (flour), polished millets, fried foods, non-vegetarian food.

The general diet that you may choose may not be the optimal one for your system as each one of us have unique requirements, imbalances as well as different metabolic rates.

A typical naturopathy diet may consist of water, fresh juices, coconut water, vegetable soups, butter milk, fruits, salads, sprouts, steamed vegetables, herbs, oilseeds, wholesome food like unpolished rice, millets.

***

# Siddha

The Siddha system of medicine has been prevalent in the ancient Tamil Nadu. The contributors of this system called the Siddhars, were mystics, yogis, poets, devotees, seers and medical men.

According to Siddha system, the individual is a microcosm of the universe. The human body consists of the five primordial elements – Earth, Water, Fire and Space, the three humours – Vatha, Pitta, Kapha and seven physical constituents. They believe that food itself is medicine and medicine itself is food. It places equal importance on body, mind and spirit and strives to restore innate harmony within the individual.

The drugs used by the Siddhas can be classified as herbal products, inorganic substances and animal products.

The therapeutic treatment consists of purgative therapy, emetic therapy, fasting therapy, steam therapy and so on.

There is also a branch dealing with traumatology and accidental injuries called Varma.

The Siddhas have also evolved a special technique for attaining spiritual awakening by arousing with yoga meditation, the kundalini Shakti (serpent power) lying dormant at the base of the spinal column in the region of the sacral plexus.

Most of the_teachings was handed over by the teacher to the disciple. Developments on the academic side and also in scientific research have been coming up.

***

# Homeopathy

Homeopathy is a pseudoscientific system of alternative medicine. It was conceived in 1796 by the German physician Samuel Hahnemann.

A basic belief behind Homeopathy is "like cures like". In other words, something that brings on the symptoms in a healthy person can, in a very small dose treat an illness with similar symptoms in a sick person. This is meant to trigger the body's natural defences. For example, red onions make your eyes water, that's why it is used in homeopathic remedies for allergies. The homeopaths weaken the ingredients by adding water or alcohol. They then shake the mixture as part of a process called potentialization. They believe this process transfers the healing essence. Lower the dose, more powerful the medicine. They come in a variety of forms like sugar pellets, liquid drops, gels and tablets. It is used for a wide variety of health issues, including some chronic illnesses.

This treatment focuses on the entire human body and based on belief that suppressing the symptoms of an illness is not the cure. Over time it can help alleviate several diseases both physiological and psychological.

***

# Yoga

India is the birth place of yoga. The development of Yoga dates back to over 5000 years. It is essentially a spiritual discipline based on an extremely subtle science, which focuses on bringing harmony between the body and the mind. The word Yoga is derived from the Sanskrit word Yuj, meaning to join or unite. Tirumalai Krishnamacharya is known as the father of modern Yoga.

 Yoga has become popular all over the world. Body, mind and soul are united through the practice of Yoga leading to ultimate salvation. Yoga also means alignment.

De crumpling of the mind can be achieved by various modulations of breath and body postures.

**Jyana Yoga** - Acquiring Wisdom and knowledge.

**Hatha Yoga** - Postures and breathing techniques.

**Karma Yoga** - Work, Science of action.

**Bhakti Yoga** - Visualize God.

**Rajya Yoga** - Meditation.

The eight limbs of Rajya Yoga are:

**Yama**: These are moral codes consisting of Truthfulness, Non-violence, No stealing, Non possessiveness and moderation in all things.

**Niyama**: A set of 5 qualities to be sought i.e., Purity, Contentment, Authority, Awareness of the Divine presence and study of sacred texts.

**Asanas**: Postures and movements designed to extend, strengthen and keep the body fully flexible and able.

**Pranayama**: The study and use of breath to aid mind and body.

**Pratyhara**: Study to gain control of mind and become aware of its hypersensitivity. Withdrawal of senses from the external world.

**Dharana**: Further stage of mind control and expansion of consciousness.

**Dhyan**: Meditation.

**Samadhi**: This is the final submit of mind, body and spirit control, the state of being one with the creator or transcendental bliss.

Some of the common Asanas help to remove toxins and metabolic wastes from the body. Regular practice strengthens the heart, lungs, muscles as well as nervous system. It helps in weight control, stamina, sound sleep, stress relief, improves mood and lowers cholesterol and high blood pressure.

Surya Namaskar or salutation to the Sun consists of a series of twelve postures practiced in a flowing sequence combining the use of the breath. It stimulates and energizes the whole body, improves circulation, strengthens arms, legs, increases spine flexibility and suppleness. It releases upper body congestion, tones and stimulates internal organs and helpful for back pain.

There are also cleansing processes which are as important as yogic exercises such as various kriyas.

Yoga is a great exercise and can be done by everyone. It can benefit anyone who remains consistent in its practice. By the practice of Yogasanas and Pranayama, you can keep your body physically, mentally and spiritually fit. In the practice of Yoga, you can express gratitude by setting an intention to appreciate every moment. When you own your breath, nobody can steal your peace.

Face yoga consists of easy exercises with your hands, and no tools are required. It can help in preventing wrinkles, crow's feet, asymmetry and unconscious creation of creases and fine lines. You can tone your face at home itself. Look out for material and apps that can guide you further.

***

# Pranayam

Pranayama is the practice of breath regulation. It is a main component of Yoga, an exercise for physical and mental wellness. In Sanskrit, Prana means life energy and Yama means control.

When you get stressed or angry – what changes is your breath. When you are totally at ease again what changes is your breath. We experience every emotion with change of breath. When you learn to navigate and manage your breath, you can navigate any situation in life.

Pranayam or yogic breathing comes after the postures and the Asanas. The control of Prana leads to control of the mind which is vital for concentration and meditation, the subsequent stages of Yoga. In Yoga breath is used to direct the flow of Prana in the body. Just as blood circulates through a network of veins and arteries, it is believed to flow through network of channels known as Nadi. There are thought to be over 72,000 of these channels crisscrossing the body. The main Nadi is along the spinal column recommending erect posture of spine. Situated along the spine are seven centers of energy known as chakras and blockages can create health problems.

The practice keeps your mind and body healthy. Deliberate deep breathing process is easy to learn and follow. It needs only some patience and continuity. If you miss out once don't let it skip again, the habit will start getting undone.

Do not breathe shallow as you will be hardly using one sixth of your lungs' intake and distribution capacities. Try and practice lesser full breaths per minute, which will improve general health, improve alertness, enhance the immune system, reduce anxiety and improve concentration.

There are various forms of Pranayama, but have three steps in common such as Inhalation, Retention, Exhalation. Sit in comfortable posture with your spine in erect position. If you have a tendency to forget or difficulty in forming a habit, do it before every meal in a method that is suitable to you, but Do it!

Some of the benefits of Pranayama are it reduces Stress, improves sleep quality, increases mindfulness, enhances cognitive performance.

***

# Mudras

Mudras are a non-verbal mode of communication and self-expression, consisting of hand gestures and finger postures.

Our body is made of five elements of nature – Earth, Water, Air, Fire, Sky. Thumb represents the Fire, Index finger the Air, Middle finger the Sky, Ring finger the Earth, Little finger represents the water. Joining these fingers with each other activates the life current to flow and correct the imbalances.

Mudras can be done by anyone and anywhere; but they are the most effective when done in meditative awareness, in meditation poses for 10 to 15 minutes to feel the result. Practicing mudras regularly can cure many ailments.

The ten most powerful hand mudras are Jyana mudra, Prithvi mudra, Vayu mudra, Shunya mudra, Surya mudra, Prana mudra, Apana mudra, Vyana Vayu mudra, Varuna mudra and Linga mudra. There are almost 400 different yogic mudras that can be practiced.

Mudras can heal Anxiety, Blood pressure, Insomnia, Weakness, Speech disorders, Improper Blood Flow, Stomach

Disorders, Headache, Hair Loss, Excessive Secretion of Hormones, Menstrual Problems, Backache, Removal of Toxins and improves body strength, helps in Concentration, Relaxation, De-addiction and much more. In additional to hand mudras, there are also:

**Mana mudras** (Head mudras) such as Nose Tip Gazing, Tongue Lock, Crow's Beak etc, which are important part of Kundalini Yoga.

**Kaya mudras** (Postural mudras) combine physical postures with breathing and concentration such as Inverted Seal, Folded mudra etc.

**Bandha mudras** (Lock mudras) are performed on the diaphragms that is respiratory, vocal and pelvic in conjunction with holding of breath in pranayama.

**Adhara mudras** (Perennial mudras) are performed on the pelvic floor area and relate to harnessing sexual energy.

There are nice apps available which tell you about mudras along with alarm and notification facilities.

***

# Reiki

Reiki means universal life force energy. We are born with it and is the best form of energy, which can be replenished. Everyone has an inherent aura or energy field which depletes due to various causes. Practitioners typically place their hands on or near the body and use their energy to affect the energy field of the person.

Energy therapies are based on the core belief in the existence of a universal life force or subtle energy that resides in and around the body.

The attunement process rejuvenates the energy centers of human body and makes them more activated. Once the Reiki channel is established one can get the energy for himself and others as and when necessary. It gives relief to an ailing or sick person. It establishes balance of energy, relieves stress and strain by reaching the root cause of diseases and cures it. It improves self-awareness and removes worries.

There is belief that energies can be balanced and harmonized using the universal healing power that every human being naturally possesses. You can give Reiki to yourself as well as others including distant Reiki.

***

# Sujok

Su means hand while Jok means palm. Developed by Prof Park Jae Woo, this therapy is safe and easy to perform. It is a Korean form of acupressure combined with reflexology.

It is also a safe method of treatment that every person can master and help himself and also others. It is based on the concept of resemblance of hands and feet to the body in their structure. The fingers and toes correspond to the whole body as well as to its separate elements.

It is very simple form of therapy involving massage to areas of the hands and feet to bring about healing reactions in the body. Do not overtax any area by working for too long or with too heavy a pressure. Ideally full treatment is given to all the areas in the hand and feet, thus treating the whole body.

Sujok therapy is known to heal mental disorders like phobia, depression, anxiety and also injuries and inflammations like Gout, Blood pressure and other skin problems.

It also makes use of seeds, semi-precious stones, chakra magnets along with pressure stimulation that help relieve problems like diabetes and kidney stones. You can also use a spiked slipper or roll on. The Sujok ring is one of the most popular items of Sujok therapy.

*Man's life depends on plants, and in turn, the life of plants is dependent on Man's activities. Owing to similar factors, people and plants enter into process of Homo interaction which guarantees them preservation, stability and development. Seed therapy can be employed by any person, but professional knowledge about the properties of various plants helps realize all potentialities of this method.*

*Prof Park Jae Woo*

In Sujok, a smile is referred as Buddha smile or child smile. Smile meditation aims to strike harmony with our mind, body and soul.

Sujok also includes treatment using Meridians, Moxa therapy, Energy balancing, Colour therapy, Tri origin properties and models and much more.

Sujok can be done along with other holistic therapies as well as medical treatments and produces no side effects.

# Anatomic Therapy

This is the art of self-treatment without taking any medicines. It was created by Healer Bhaskar through his extensive research and expertise. All parts of the body are dependent on blood; hence the quality and quantity of the blood are the fundamental reasons for all the diseases in our body.

It is understanding the body's language and by correcting our mistakes we can support the body's doctor to cure almost all diseases. All required medicines are available in fruits, vegetables, food, water Air for most internal diseases. According to this system also our body is made up of the five elements namely land, water, air, fire and space and by regulating them we can lead a happy life. To secrete pure blood there is need to eat and drink water properly, breathe, and rest. It also includes taste therapy such as Sweet, Salty, Bitter, Pungent, Astringent – each having its own taste, primary actions and common sources. There are no diet restrictions.

This therapy is known to be effective in cases such as Diabetes, Blood pressure, Thyroid, Headache, Eye problems, Sinus, Tonsils, Memory loss, Irritable bowel syndrome, Backache including Cancer and AIDS.

# Neuro Linguistic Programming (NLP)

NLP is Neuro Linguistic Programming. Neuro stands for our neurological responses and linguistic for the language and programming of our patterns and responses. NLP is said to have been originated by Richard Bandler from the University of California.

The three principles of NLP are:

✓ Cause and Effect.

✓Perception is projection.

✓ Responsibility for value.

Some of the pre suppositions are that everyone has a unique model of the world, people are not their behaviors and that every behavior is useful in some context. If one person can do something, anyone can learn and do it. The quality of our life is determined by the quality of our communication. Positive changes always come from adding resources. People are map makers. People's maps are made up of pictures, sounds, feelings, smells and tastes. If you change your map, you will change your emotional state. Choice is better than no choice. If what you are doing is not working, do something else.

There is the Wellness Model, Representational Systems, The Chunking Exercise and much more.

The known benefits of practice of NLP techniques are:

✓ Clarity of vision, purpose and values
✓ Overcoming limited beliefs
✓ Enhanced self confidence
✓ Managing difficult people
✓ Developing new strategies
✓ Dealing with pain and allergies
✓ Building your personal success system
✓ Managing our emotional states
✓ Future pacing

NLP permits you to evolve and change your habits as to how you want to be. It is a tool that will help you with your holistic development and to be able to communicate clearly.

***

# Autogenic Training

Autogenic Training is a technique of Self Hypnosis developed by H H Sultz, a German Neurologist. The technique consists of a series of six mental exercises used to elicit the bodily sensations of warmth and heaviness. This has the effect of producing the physiological changes of the relaxation response. It is a technique that teaches your body to respond to your verbal commands. These commands tell your body to relax and help control breathing, blood pressure, heart beat, and body temperature. The goal is to achieve deep relaxation and reduce stress.

Conditions such as social Anxiety Disorder, Depression and Insomnia can benefit from Autogenic Training.

Through the use of breathing techniques, specific verbal stimuli, and mindful meditation, Autogenic Training can help people seeking treatment to reduce stress and achieve relaxation of body and mind.

There are six stages; inducing heaviness, inducing warmth, the heart practice, breathing exercise, abdominal practice and head practice.

***

# Other Therapies

- Hypnotherapy.

- Lama Fera.

- Feng shui.

- Merkaba healing.

- Pranic healing.

- Past life regression.

- Physiotherapy.

- Redikall healing.

- Gems & Crystals.

- Acupuncture.

- Magnetic healing.

- Chelation therapy.

and many more which you can check out for greater details as they appeal to you.

# *Chapter 11:*
# *Spiritual Health Management*

Happiness can be material or spiritual. In material happiness our desires are met. In spiritual happiness we outgrow the desire itself.

If we keep spending our life generating debts, we get trapped in the cycle of birth and death. The best way is stop generating debt, outgrow hunger, fear, craving for wealth and power and vices and attain tranquility or in other words "Moksha".

The object is to keep the lamp of our inner life burning brightly. Don't let it get extinguished.

It is not impermanence that makes us suffer. What makes us suffer is wanting things to be permanent, whereas it is not designed to be that way.

We must have certain fundamental virtues before we can make any headway in our spiritual life. If our mind is filled with noble thoughts, we will not find ourselves lonely and unprotected at any time.

Spiritual power means creating only those thoughts which are positive and necessary in any situation. Anything unresolved within our energy field will keep manifesting itself in your life until you heal it.

## Commencement of Inner Journey.

Make yourself ready for the change.

Checking your actions and then changing them should be a natural habit and not something that is a burden on the mind. Perform good actions that will give you happiness first, and to others after that.

For those who are on the spiritual path, being alone, keeping a distance from people, and becoming silent, are not issues, these are opportunities.

Find answers to your questions. Learn from observing Nature.

Visit holy places and shrines that appeal to you.

Find peace with yourself. Connect with your soul. Various tools are Meditation, Singing, Community Songs, Prayers etc. Have your own unique mantra for all occasions.

Give back knowledge you attain in some form or another back to the society. Find happiness in happiness of others.

The living, have awareness of death and hence there is yearning for life, hunger for food, safety concerns and greater desires. Focus on controlling and restricting unnecessary desires. The concept of value exists only among humans, based on the meaning we give it.

Anything you can't control is teaching you how to let go. Don't resist beyond a point, accept the flow.

***

# Meditation

It is the art of mental quietness and can be achieved by withdrawing all thoughts from all directions and focusing on a single point or object.

In Meditation, the first step is to overcome disturbances of the body. It is difficult for most people to sit comfortably for more than a short period, without feeling pain or wanting to stretch. This causes the awareness to be externalized whereas the aim is to direct the awareness inwards to the working of the mind. The next step is to try and achieve calmness of mind and relaxation. Normally people have a mind like a stormy sea.

We must begin with being aware of one object, symbol or thing to the exclusion of everything else. This pointed attention allows the awareness to pierce and enter the various depths of the mind. A silent tranquil mind makes you listen various voices from the depth of the mind which you can't catch otherwise. The mind becomes a receptor of bliss and wisdom, since all this arises naturally when the mind is in the state of inner silence.

An ordinary person gets thousands of thoughts per day. When you practice meditation, you reduce the number of thoughts drastically and develop an organized thought pattern. Dive deep into your sub conscious mind in meditation, come out with beautiful pearls of wisdom and hidden talents.

Meditation is the pure form of trance that no alcohol or substance can give. Unwanted thoughts which are a mental baggage have to be removed, de-clutter yourself of them as often as you can.

Evolve from lower to higher consciousness. See the invisible. Despite there being so much to see, closing your eyes and looking within is Apex. Feel the tangible. Achieve what once looked like near impossible.

Sit in a straight-backed position and gently close your eyes. Inhale deeply and exhale calmly. Become increasingly aware of the breathing movements as you inhale and exhale. As you inhale, take in fresh breath, good energy, joy; and as you exhale, let go of all stale negative energy, stress and sorrow. Feel refreshed.

'Zero zone' is an appointment of the mind with the soul – reach out and be there. Feel the calmness. Be enlightened.

There are many guided meditation programs too where you can affirm that your energy fields are getting repaired, life force is being replenished, the body is getting stronger and healthier and sense of well-being is being restored. Welcome new ideas into yourself.

The union between the human spirit and the divine can be reached through spiritual insight, independent of reason and senses. In the larger perspective of the cosmos and our connection with it, we are all united. The all-pervasive Supreme soul is connected with our spirit and this realization can be experienced through meditation. It is a powerful tonic. Try to develop both intellect and intuition.

Each soul has its journey. If we take our earthly journey as a mission to self-improvement then march on regardless. Meditation and spiritual seeking, is a personal journey of the soul. It should not be imposed and each one has to find the way one is most comfortable with.

Spirituality is knowing the universal self in you. Seek and you will find your Guide who will help you reach there. He may be a human being, a book, or you yourself. Attempt to change your perceptions about life completely – and try to connect accordingly.

When material, psychological and spiritual dimensions in a person are brought into balance, life becomes whole. It is the process that unlocks the door of the supreme abode of immortal bliss. It destroys all causes of sorrow.

Sometimes, when you are happy doing what you are, with intense concentration, you get automatically into a state of meditation as a function of happiness.

See life energy as the river of your life, which should flow through your body dynamically. You can also meditate on various colors or the infinite space, waterfalls, rain drops or universal love.

***

# Chakra Meditation

Chakra Meditation is designed to bring you back to neutrality so as to place a balance. Chakras are essentially your energy centers. There are total of seven chakras:

**Crown Chakra:** Colour – Purple; located on the top of the head which is the center of Enlightenment and Spirituality Consciousness.

**Third Eye Chakra:** Colour – Indigo; located between the eyebrows which is the center of Intuition and Understanding.

**Throat Chakra:** Colour – Blue; located in center base of neck which is the center of Communication and Self Expression.

**Heart Chakra:** Colour – Green; located in center of chest which is the center of Balance, Love and Connection.

**Solar Plexus Chakra:** Colour – Yellow; located below the Sternum which is the center for Energy, Vitality, Will Power, Desire and Personal Authority.

**Sacral Chakra:** Colour – Orange; located below the Navel which is the center of Relationships, Emotions and Sexuality.

 **Root Chakra:** Colour – Red; located at the base of the spine which is the center of Survival, Self-preservation and feeling of Being Grounded.

Meditation becomes a protective aura into which no negative energy can penetrate.

***

# *Chapter 12:*
# *Common Distractions/Hurdles*

## Id / Procrastination

Have you noticed how sometimes, when you are just about to do a constructive activity, something inside of you just stops you from doing it like applying a brake for no good reason; or simply by a wave of lethargy? When you know you must do something important and yet don't do it, which is the art of delaying and postponing something. Identify and get rid of this tendency. Develop a counter force to tackle it.

***

## Ego

It is a person's sense of self-esteem or self-importance. Being important comes from the ego and being happy comes from the soul. Attitude and ego are self-created. People carry the huge burden called ego which creates a false identity about oneself; like I am so & so, I should be loved, I need to be respected, I need to be invited, etc., sometimes even before one has achieved anything worthwhile or is able to claim a position or accomplishment in life. People get irritated instantly by others' actions or words, which could come from friends, parents, children, colleagues or spouses; and instant sparks of anger are ignited and one starts fuming. Avoid it.

There is this comparison with others in beauty, wealth, lifestyle, marks, talent and appraisals. One should not get disturbed and insecure; rather we must be grateful with what we have and develop ourselves.

***

# Temper

Results of Anger are more painful than the reasons of anger. Holding anger eats you from the inside.

Anger is a defensive feeling meant to protect our deeper feelings such as hurt, guilt, fear, insecurity and frustration.

Detach yourself from annoyance, be aloof to it. Harsh words are best ignored. Be more tolerant, and let many such things just pass by you.

Break the mood, change your activity, leave the room when you feel you are about to lose your cool.

Try to rearrange situations so that other people's reactions or past reactions no more upsets you.

Discover your self-defeating patterns and self-concepts. The body will produce hormones and chemicals which will destroy you at cellular level and a mental level. Stay calm, smile and change to another happy thought.

***

# Possessiveness

It is the excessive desire to possess or dominate, including the excessive desire to acquire or possess more material wealth than one needs or deserves. We all are rolling stones. It is mine, It is theirs; are too petty issues when we look at mankind through the prism of a peripatetic context and entity. We are all migrants. No one has an exclusive hold over a place, territory, language and other specifications. The trees show us how lovely it is to let things go. Just reflect.

*** 

# Static Comfort Zone

A comfort zone is a beautiful place, but nothing grows there. If we have to be successful in life we must not permanently reside in our comfort zone but must venture out and reach greater heights and newer zones. Your brilliance awaits you on the edge of your comfort zone. Explore it and live the life that you have dreamt about.

*** 

# Misinformation

A fact is information minus emotion. An opinion is information plus experience. Ignorance is opinion lacking information and stupidity is an opinion that ignores a fact.

Read widely, think deeply and retain your sense of discrimination. Don't be distracted by the noise of misinformation.

Lack of communication often leads to misinformation.

***

# Whiling Away Time

Don't just sit in a corner of your room and allow yourself to be cornered into depression and anxiety. Keep doing something like reading, playing music or watching your favorite show. You can master this as a habit by practicing it till you achieve consistency. Take rest breaks only after you really feel tired or your work at hand is completed. Time is like a snowflake; it melts away while we try to decide what to do with it, so beware.

***

# Drifting / Distractions

Mind is a winged entity. It will fly off in a whisker. Keep yourself consciously grounded. Awareness is the first step to change. Distractions are traps that pull our attention away from what is really important and what really adds to our happiness. Starve your distractions and feed your focus.

You can't do big things if you are distracted by small things. How true!

***

# Inconsistency

This is the cause for much failure and prevention of attaining full potential. Keep getting back to focus and cruise along. Positive affirmations are helpful.

A Wise Man can learn more from a foolish question than a Fool can learn from a wise answer.

River breaks the rock not because it is strong, because it is persistent.

Every lost game inspires us to try one more time. We must remember defeat is temporary, but giving up makes it permanent.

***

# Lack of Confidence

Often our minds are split. The conscious mind wants to move forward but the sub conscious mind is afraid of losing something to which it is attracted. This ambivalence shows itself as a lack of confidence.

There could be a number of causes leading to lack of confidence. Many a times one is a first timer in life. When you start achieving success, many will try and bring you down in life by creating hurdles and even discouraging you. Don't let such actions ever effect you adversely.

Some changes look negative on the surface but you will soon realize that space is being created in your life for something new to emerge. Being still, looking and listening activates the non-conceptual intelligence within you. Let stillness direct your words and action.

Look back and get experience, look forward and see hope. Look around and find reality. Look within and find confidence.

# Overreaction

Understand the facts in the correct perspective. Give a measured response at your end.

Don't react to everything that bothers you. The best sign of maturity is to walk away, rather than getting even. Reacting to things that upset you gives someone else power over your emotions. Life is better when you focus on what is happening inside you than around you.

Pay attention when people react with hostility to your boundaries. Find the edge where their respect for you ends.

***

# Vices and Addictions

Television and to a greater extent smart mobile phones add value to your life but don't excessively indulge in their use and kill your time without any take away. Push it to the background whenever the possible. A day wasted will never come back; don't follow the crowd mentality.

Alcohol and smoking can be habit forming and must be very controlled if not totally eradicated.

 Drug abuse substances are a big NO, it just destroys life and families and it is often a one way journey to DOOMSDAY. Addiction is a family disease as one or two people may use it, but the whole family suffers due to the havoc created.

***

# Energy Burn Out

Exercise according to your capacity, do not over burn yourself.

Identify the vitamins and minerals you are deficient in and take remedial steps with a doctor's advice and prescription.

Speak when necessary. Avoid getting angry. Limit your thoughts. Get rid of persistent unwanted thoughts or bad experiences. Have your moments of silence. The energy it takes to react to every bad thing that happens to you, drains you and stops you from seeing the other good things in life. Conserve your energies and use them sparingly. Try and harness the potential; spiritually make an attempt to dive deeper into the cosmic world.

***

# Social Media Overkill

This is of recent origin and can actually do more harm than good if not exercising restraint. Push these activities to the background. What you post in social media is the reflection of your mind to some extent. When people react to it, they may be also in different frames of mind. There are countless apps today for a single requirement.

The best way to appreciate something is to be without it for a while. Allocate time and don't keep it on limitlessly.

Use electronic gadgets sparingly as radiation affects supply of oxygen to the brain.

***

## Optimism Bias

It the belief that each one of us is more likely to experience good outcomes and less likely to experience bad outcomes. The key to optimism bias is that we disregard the reality of an overall situation because we think we are excluded from the potential negative effects.  Steer clear of it and be alive to the situation at hand. Anything can happen to anyone at any time with or without a warning. The best example was the Corona Virus or casualties as practically no one was sure who would survive and who would not.

***

# The Devil Inside Us

It includes the negativity committee, the jealous competitor, superficial judge, the cheater and the victim card holder.

Most of the time we tame our demons; at other times, they tame us.

The devil inside often tries to release evil by making one react recklessly. Be careful of taking extreme steps. Don't be self-destructive and don't mess up.

Attempt to be moderate, out of which pure happiness springs.

***

## Judgmental Mind

Once we have pre-judged someone, it prevents inspiration, grace and our higher mind functioning.

The complete picture is often missing. We tend to judge anyone who does not live up to our ideals. When the ego judges, someone has to sacrifice.

You need to stop explaining yourself to people who are motivated by selfishness and narrow levels of perception.

***The judgmental mind is a double-edged sword, it cuts both ways, it cuts you, it cuts others***

*- Osho*

***

# Mind Poison

Anything far beyond we need may become poison for us. This could be power, laziness, food, ego, ambition, vanity, fear, anger or anything else.

Poisonous thoughts must not be nurtured against anyone or your own self.

Pay no attention to toxic words. What people say is often a reflection of themselves, not you.

***

# *Chapter 13:*
# *Your Trusted Comrades*

## You Yourself (Self Belief)

Your real life-partner is your own body. Even the greatest mind cannot think for another, because it does not know the entire situation, both external and internal. We cannot give a true picture to anyone no matter how hard we try. There is a way of finding our own solution and that is by learning to enter into our own depth zone.

Don't be hard on yourself. The quieter you become, the more you are able to hear. Become self-made ASAP. Stop blaming yourself for every situation. Don't pity yourself. Meet the little devil in yourself, face and encounter it and make it very weak. Surround yourself with positivity. Invest in yourself wisely.

First think, then speak. Because of lack of patience or impulsiveness, you may lose out on many things even without realizing it.

You are only responsible for how you behave in response to other people's behavior. Also do not accept others blaming you for their own inadequacies or laziness.

When you speak the truth, you don't have to remember what you said.

Visualization is a potent tool for actualization of your dreams; slowly you will find new thoughts and ideas stimulating you, giving you creative ideas to handle situations. Assertiveness is a way of expressing your true feelings in an appropriate manner, which makes you feel confident and in control of the situation.

Eliminate unwanted habits, observe how they try to control you and note their frequency. Reward yourself daily if you are able to reinforce new good habits.

An impaired self-esteem can be restored, learn from your failures. Give it all it takes. Look inwards when you need support not essentially towards external beings.

If we take care of the moments, the years will take care of themselves. Similarly take care of minor things in life and major things will get taken care of by themselves.

Be thankful for closed doors, detours, and roadblocks. They protect you from paths and places not meant for you.

Beliefs are the mental bandwidth of your perception, performance and action. Limiting beliefs confines, restricts and hampers your life. Re-examine all your beliefs in the light of present moment and accept or replace them.

Your intuition is your natural gift that can double your efficiency at work, guide you in your life, and set you on your purpose. Always trust your instincts, they are messages from your soul. Don't allow your emotions to overpower your intelligence.

There won't always be supporters. At times, you have to clap for yourself. Don't feel ashamed to do so.

***

## Close Family

Everything around us is temporary. Humans are good at adapting to adverse circumstances. One can imagine how our ancestors must have faced so many difficult situations in their lifetimes. The pipelines were laid by your ancestors the benefits of which you enjoy today. In the end, it is your own home and immediate family that keep you safe. To take care of those who once cared for us is one of the higher honors.

Family is mostly blood related, but not always, as exceptions do exist.

***

## Books

Your choice of Books is very important. Serious reading connects you with the most inspiring people and you can benefit from their experiences. Books can actually guide you, if you look at reading with a view to seek solutions by means of simple or even cryptic clues. Read with an open mind. Books are often described as Man's Best Friends. Every time you read your favorite book, though the contents remain same, new perceptions get added.

*You know you have read a good book when you turn the last page and feel a little sad as if you have lost a friend*

*- Paul Sweeney*

***

# God and Your Prayers

The glory of the Supreme is beyond mind and speech. Let us give our inner being a chance to listen to the voice which is too subtle for the physical ear to hear.

God is infinite and all-abiding. Trust in him.

God answers your prayers through interaction with others, look for the signs and symbolism that would need some finer observation and attention. It is a personal connect between the two.

In your prayers forgive people who hurt you in the past, not because they necessarily deserve it but because you deserve your happiness.

Prayer is not a spare wheel that you pull out when in trouble, but it is a steering wheel that directs the right path throughout life, be consistent.

Whenever an unexpected joy passes through your heart and suddenly you smile for no reason, remember someone somewhere wishes you to be happy.

Each day have one good thought and one good deed to start with.

The answers you seek never come when the mind is busy, they come when the mind is still.

God has strange ways of looking after his creations. You can sometimes use the power of your visualization for understanding it.

There are many phenomena in our living environment and outside which are beyond our normal conception and understanding.

***

# Humans

The other being is either a predator, prey, rival or mate to put it crudely. It is important whom you trust. Even the smallest lie can break the biggest trust.

Each life is a radiating power, which has either a good or bad influence.

No humans can keep secrets forever. Avoid sharing your secrets, they will sooner or later find their way into the super marketplace with various price tags.

When common trouble is faced by a group the unity will be more compared to an individual facing personal low. Everyone you meet is generally interested to know what career you pursue, your marital status, children, house, properties and slowly the list becomes endless. Hardly ever anyone asks if you are happy (Health Ledger). It is so important to Love someone and a little bit extra on their bad days. We can't help everyone, but everyone can help someone.

Reflect also upon the many people who invisibly touch your life every day, who have directly or indirectly helped you some time or the other and look out for your update.

Focus on your own voice, it is the one that matters most. Start to develop it if you haven't yet.

*There is nothing so useless as doing effectively that which should not be done at all*

*- Peter Drucker*

***

# Effective Time Management

Time management is a set of common-sense skills that helps to use time in the most effective and productive way possible; and our values reflect on our priorities. Realize the value of each second.

Set goals correctly, prioritize wisely, set time limits, organize yourself, remove non-essential tasks and keep planning ahead.

*Time is the only capital that any human has, and the only thing he can't afford to lose*

*- Albert Einstein*

***

# Sense of Humor, Laughter and Happiness

Everyone must try to develop a sense of humor. Watch laughter series and such talk shows. Look back at the days when you were happy go lucky and joyful.

Laughter therapy helps in smooth blood circulation, discharge of body toxins, oozing out useful hormones. It can also help you to reduce pain and prevent infections. You can go ahead and join a Laughter Club if you wish to. The sound of laughter travels from heart to heart and lights innumerable candles on the way.

When you give happiness to others, it will find its way back to you. Spread happiness.

Life is a series of mirth and laughter, if one had an eye for the humorous aspects of human behavior.

Sitting quietly or following our true purpose allows happiness to come to us naturally.

***

## Recreational Activity

This can be anything that can soothe your soul. Identify such activities if you have not done so, it is never too late. You just need to start and keep it going. You may have multiple aptitudes pursue all of those that you possibly can. You decide.

These can be hiking, camping, hunting, fishing, rafting, sailing, biking, rock climbing, skiing, golfing, gardening, indoor games and scores of others.

*If bread is the first necessity of life, recreation is a close second*

*- Edward Bellamy*

***

## Your Communication

Communication is the bridge between two parties, on which both can win in a mature and more integrated fashion. Be discerning rather than naive. It is also important to communicate willingness to learn and change. Slowly become an expert in effective communication.

Listen, talk straight, have emotional control over verbal communication.

Look out for non-communicative gestures and visual communication as well.

All great world leaders have been excellent communicators.

***

# Silence

A silent being is a very restful being. Even in a household we find that a person who is calm, composed and thoughtful radiates a powerful influence. One may be alone, communicating with his inner self. Silence has a wonderful creative power. Silent relaxation will definitely have a very beneficial effect on our physical, mental and moral being. What sleep does for our body and nervous system, silence does for our mind and spirit. Our thoughts grow undisturbed and uninterrupted on the silent soil of the mind. The practice of silence also has a profound significance when we embrace the spiritual life.

***

# Optimism

An optimist can always see the light at the end of the tunnel. He hopes for the best. Optimism nurtures hope and cheerfulness. It strengthens the will to survive calamities.

People with a happy cheery nature have a beam in their eyes and their bright disposition helps them to carry the burdens of life with a smile.

Optimism aids patience, increases energy and positivity. Everyone likes the company of such an optimistic person.

***

# Forgiveness

Many people are scared to forgive as forgiving is associated with being a victim, which is actually just not the case. It is forgiveness that changes perception and experience which changes the very pattern that initiated the problem. Our forgiveness of others releases our buried guilt.

It is important to understand that 'Letting Go' is not a weakness but a blessing we can give ourselves more than to anyone. Forgiveness does not change the past, but it does enlarge the future.

The weak can never forgive. Forgiveness is the attribute of the strong. Always forgive your enemies. The wise forgive but do not forget.

***

# *Chapter 14:*
# *Social Responsibility/Benevolent Activities*

Have you ever given someone a motivational speech while you were hurting on the inside? That is strength.

We make a living by what we get, but we make a life by what we give.

Always undertake noble, charitable activities with a pure mind. Some of them could be:

- **Basic Expenses:** Provide basic expenses for food, survival expenses, for the poor and needy.

- **Donate old belongings:** Clothing, bedding items, heaters, cycles, anything useful lying idle with you.

- **Education expenses:** For the young, elderly, socially downtrodden and poor.

- **Medical Expenses:** Emergency medical treatment for the needy as well as for prolonged diseases.

- **Natural calamity:** Give relief goods, medical aids, temporary shelters, evacuation assistance, assist in fund raising.

- **Blood donation:** All healthy people can do it, usually every three months.

- **Organ Donation:** It is also a concept fast gaining recognition, though it is ultimately one's own personal choice to give someone a new lease of life.

- **Sponsor a Child:** School and college fees, Job placement assistance, Encouragement of talent such as in music, arts, sports. Help a student to find scholarship. Sponsor a visit to amusement park, gift a library your old books. Organize a class on computer skills.

- **Interest free loan:** One can start from helping their own employees at least for house, transport and small-scale business. Pay off some debt if possible.

- **Free samples:** Give some of your business products for free to the needy and NGOs.

- **Hospital:** Offer free services, donate wheel chairs or essential needs. Distribute sweets on festivals.

- **Orphanage:** Sponsor a good meal, birthday celebrations, new clothes, visit to a theatre or picnic.

- **Prison:** Donate whatever is permissible, sponsor a good dish, get sweets distributed.

- **Home for the elderly**: Spend time with them. Bring small gifts. Celebrate their special days.

- **Free Professional service:** Free medical, legal, financial consultation, counseling, use of technological gadgets including smartphones.

- **Use of social media:** If you are a blogger or social media influencer, voice out for the poor and needy.

- **Animal Care**: Take care of stray pets and other animals. Get an injured animal treated.  Sponsor a pet vacation.

- **Preservation of nature:** Don't add to the pollution. Make your own little contribution. Plant trees. Save water.

- **Pray for the less privileged:** It is free of cost and everyone and anyone can do it for the entire humanity and world at large by Individual or community prayers.

- **Spread Peace and Love:** By your thoughts, actions and deeds which is limitless. Take free lectures, write articles or books.

Social service is the most fulfilling of all activities. When you give back to the society and nature, it gives you a great inner sense of happiness. One person can make a difference and everyone should try.

*Every Man is guilty of the good things he did not do.*

*- Voltaire*

# Chapter 15:
# *Karma, Purpose, Guide*

## Law of Karma

Karma means action – It comes from Sanskrit root 'kree' meaning 'to do.'

The vibe you put out; is the vibe you get back. Karma means action as well as reaction to that action. Reactions to past actions create the circumstances that you encounter in your present life.

The Universe is not punishing or blessing you with Karma. It is responding to the vibrational energy you are sending out. Be mindful of what you bring into existence. It will certainly come back to you someday sooner or later.

Life is neither pain nor otherwise; it is just the running account of your own past deeds. Lessons in life will be repeated until they are learned.

All the things that are not in control are born out of past actions. Bad things happen to the best of the people for circumstances beyond their control. Suffer with inner strength and resilience.

Sorrow and pain must be accepted and owned with grace. There are no true tragedies, only lessons.

Whatever is taken away will be replaced with something better. Never have regrets in life.

Create rings of positivity around your thoughts, actions, deeds and leave the rest. Don't try to force changes in other people lives, they are governed by their respective karmas.

The World is a combination of Time, Action, and Cause. Every action has a reaction. When your finger gets cut with a knife, blood oozes out immediately. Here the reaction is instantaneous. There is no time gap whatsoever. On the other hand, food we eat takes at least two hours to be digested. Take the case of a seed. A seed sown today takes two to three days to sprout. Here the time gap is slightly more as compared to the previous instance. It takes years for a sapling to grow into a gigantic tree and yield fruits. Thus, the time gap between action and reaction may vary depending upon the nature of action. It is not possible to say when, how, and where one will face the consequences of one's action, but for sure, none can escape the repercussion of their actions.

***

# Purpose of Life

Life is a journey with problems to solve and lessons to learn. We have apparently come here to undergo certain reformatory procedures, that is practically what life seems to suggest.

Just imagine from a free soul you become caged in a body with severe limitations for a lifetime in this earthly world. We come here and start thinking we will be here forever. We build houses, properties beyond our basic needs, but neglect our karmas which we are going to carry to where we came from and into our future births. Our journey is about being more deeply involved in life and yet less attached to it. Develop your consciousness to the fullest extent and achieve perfection and peace. Find a new outlook, value yourself, and start to live differently.

Know the difference between simply existing and truly living by redefining your aims and daily objectives.

Take a day at a time and do your best and leave the rest.

Life is too short to worry about haters. They don't deserve to be an issue in your life. Think about the people who love and support you. It's a beautiful feeling, when someone tells you, "I wish I knew you earlier."

Regrets and bitterness hold you back. The past cannot be changed. Life only ever moves forward.

Focus on deeper things that will really count toward a happy life.

Doing good for someone is like making fixed deposit in God's bank. You may not be able to calculate the interest, but he does and he will give it back to you, when you need it the most.

A problem arises when we equate our purpose with goal-based achievements. The Universe is not interested in that, but your heart. When you choose kindness, compassion and love, you are already aligned with your true purpose.

Even most Atheists and Agnostics believed in underlying forces of good and evil.

***

# Guides

Your life guides can be your books, music, instinct, knowledge, outlook acquired or knowledge. You have to face the situation that you know best and you need to hone those skills and be alive to the process to be the master of your life. Don't forget how amazing and unique you are. Love yourself. Invoke your inner wisdom. You can as well avail the services of your support system, belief system, elders, friends, a formal Guru if you wish, but stay quiet rather than explaining your problems to people who are just curious and don't really care. Time has a way of showing us what really matters in life. No action is also an action.

Just as there are family Doctors and Lawyers, we need more family Counselors and Psychologists integral with greater connect to the society at large. A life coach can do for you what a personal trainer does for your physical fitness.

I believe in Denmark and few other countries there exists a project of a library where you can borrow a person instead of a book to listen to their life story for thirty minutes. Listening to their story makes you realize how much you should not judge a book by its cover.

***

# Chapter 16:

# In Pursuit Of Happiness

Win or lose, Life has to go on. Happiness is when, what you think, what you say and what you do are in harmony. Everyone deserves happiness.

You need to firstly create an intention to be happy and create a bubble of happiness deep inside. Offer yourself affirmations of kindness, healing and love.

Ultimately happiness rests on how you establish a solid sense of self or being. Happiness does not lie in outward appearances nor in vanity. It is a matter of how you feel inside. It is a deep resonance in your life, to be filled each day with a rewarding sense of exhilaration and purpose, a sense of tasks accomplished and of deep fulfillment. People who feel this way are truly happy. Those who have this sense of satisfaction even if they are extremely busy are much happier than those who have time on their hands but feel empty inside.

It takes a great deal of maturity to realize that everything happens for the best. Many of us go through major lessons, challenges, trials and tests throughout our lifetime.

*In simple terms, the secret to living well and longer is: Eat half, Walk double, Laugh triple and Love without measure*

*- An Ancient Proverb*

Happiness is like a remote control; we lose it every time. We go crazy looking for it and many times without knowing it, we are sitting on top of it. The art of being happy, is to be satisfied with what you have. You glow differently when you are actually happy. If you are looking for happiness in life, find out what you love the most, fill the mind with it, make it a part of daily schedule. Soon you will discover the real you from within.

The real sorrow in life is not about getting sick, old or having to die, for we come across many such people who are happy. Many have lost their sensitivity to pain.

Be ready for the change. Low happiness index results in negative thought patterns, stimulus of Neuro endocrinal glands leading to secretion of Cortisol, Gonadotropins, increasing thyroid stimulating hormones. These hormones cause changes in metabolism of body cells. Each and every organ goes through changes, leading to Diabetes, Obesity, Hair Loss, Loss of Energy, Libido, Poor Healing, Poor Absorption, Loss of Youthfulness causing Pre-Mature Ageing.

When you have a positive and happy thought pattern, due to your balanced life style, happy hormones are released. Happy hormones are serotonin, dopamine, ghrelin, oxytocin, melatonin etc. Once you have plenty of these hormones rushing into your blood stream, you get happiness, feeling of everlasting power and joy.

You live longer once you realize that time spent being unhappy is wasted and you can't get back your precious time lost, for a second use.

Learn the art of happiness thinking, in the worst of situations find a thought which is happy and stay with it, stay blissful inside. Endorphins are released by exercise, watching funny stuff brings forth laughter. Dopamine is released when we achieve our little and big tasks. Serotonin is released when we act in a way that benefits others. Oxytocin is released when we are close to human beings.

Reduce the number of thoughts of the idle mind. Change the negative thoughts by positive thoughts immediately.

Everything we do is for either running away from pain or moving toward pleasure, but it is not so simple. For example, cigarette smoking gives instant pleasure to a smoker, but there is pain too lurking somewhere beneath for certain imminent life-threatening situation that may develop.

Sometimes one has to accept the things as they are. Do not lose happiness at any cost.

There is no greater wealth in this world than peace of mind. People who shine from within don't need the spot light.

De-clutter your life, get rid of unwanted things. Quit nonessential groups on social media, avoid confrontation and controversy. In a few days you will notice how you may have some more space around. Your forgotten smile will be back.

Today deleting is more essential than adding on. Checkout your contacts on social networks and keep evaluating each one. Not everyone deserves to be on your hot list.

Life is full of painful and happy experiences. Life is too short to argue and fight. Don't wait for things to get better. Life will always be complicated. Learn to be happy right now, otherwise you will run out of time. Count on your blessings.

Value your close ones and move on with your head held high and a smile for everyone.

Life itself has no meaning; it is an opportunity to create a meaning. Go where you feel most alive.

Happiness is intrinsic, it is an internal thing. When you build it on to yourself, no external circumstances can take it away.

Forgiveness is the intentional and voluntary process by which a victim undergoes a change in feeling and attitude regarding an offence. Have the ability to wish the offender well.

Every dark cloud has a silver lining. Every negative effect has a positive beginning. Sometimes silence is the best way to communicate your emotions.

Begin the inward journey. Try therapeutic surrender, it helps to see things the way they are, and not an exaggerated version of things.

Peace of mind is a beautiful gift, which can give to ourselves just by expecting nothing from anyone. Learn the art of enjoying the empty spaces; leave spaces in your daily schedule, give space to every relationship.

Now make your Rules!!

*Be so happy that when others look at you, they become happy too. Let us be grateful to the people who make us happy, they are the charming gardeners who make our souls blossom.*

*- Marcel Proust*

Within you there must be a stillness and a sanctuary to which you can retreat at any time and be yourself.

Relax, slow down a bit. Don't take things personally. Don't take life too seriously. The beautiful thing about life is that you can always change, grow and get better. You aren't defined by your past. You aren't your mistakes either.

The best things in life are the people you love, the places you've seen, and the memories you've made along the way – treasure them.

Science has not been able to explain an infinite number of phenomena; why certain things happen in a certain way, but we all have power within us to make ourselves happy. All we need to do is to utilize that power.

***

# SAMPLE QUESTIONNAIRE

Q1. Have you tried understanding yourself and others?

Q2. Do you work smarter or just harder?

Q3. Do you take care of your physical, mental and spiritual health?

Q4. Were you a good child /parent?

Q5. Are you loyal towards your family, profession, peers and to yourself?

Q6. Do you follow a routine?

Q7. Do you strive for excellence?

Q8. Do you have constructive hobbies?

Q9. How do you treat your subordinates?

Q10. How often to you exercise and meditate?

Q11. Do you lose your temper often?

Q12. Have you been cheated by the very ones you trusted?

Q13. How many trees you have planted so far?

Q14. How many children's education was sponsored by you?

Q15. Do you put trash in Dust bins or in the open?

Q16. Do you contribute in saving water and electricity?

Q17. How many broken homes have you helped recover?

Q18.  How many animals have you adopted?

Q19. How many times have you forgiven your adversary?

Q20. How many times have you broken your promises?

Q21. Did you do your duties at workplace and home diligently?

Q22. Do you feed birds?

Q23. Did you try to connect with your inner self?

Q24. Have you helped people resolve their issues?

Q25. How many people have you made to smile?

Q26. Have you been considerate to the Sick and infirm?

Q27. Do you learn from your mistakes?

Q28. Do you constantly try and improve yourself?

Q29. Have you discharged your basic duties and commitments?

Q30. Are you considerate towards mental health patients?

Q31. Have you tried giving up your negative traits?

Q32. Have you listed out your benevolent works that can make you count as a good person?

Q33. Did you give your relationships a second chance of survival?

Q34. Do you prepare a Balance Sheet of your good and bad
       deeds?

**Make your own exhaustive questions, answer them
truthfully and review your responses.

***

# NOTES